Simple CERAMICS

HAND-BUILT POTS FOR KITCHEN AND GARDEN

DAWNA RICHARDSON-HYDE

Lothian
BOOKS

Dedication

To David, Nyssa-Jane and Christopher, who put up with a grumpy wife and mother when failed pieces came out of the kiln, an absent Mum for many school holidays, and a desperate Mum when deadlines became tight!

And to all my students past and present, who share my love and excitement for clay, glaze, firing and kilns!

Acknowledgements

To Sara Gowan for typing and proofing the manuscript.

To my colleague Kevin Boyd at Outer Easter TAFE, without whose collaborative teaching and idea-sharing, the seeds of this book would have taken much longer to germinate.

To Outer Eastern College of TAFE, Wantirna South, Victoria, for the use of its beautiful gardens to photograph the garden pieces, and to the Horticulture Department for the donation of plants for the photos.

To Lindsay Farr from The Bonsai Farm, Mt Dandenong, Victoria, for the tortured bonsai tree.

To Janet England for her support and commitment to the craft in Australia.

To Will Mulder of Clayworks for his technical advice.

A Lothian Book

Thomas C. Lothian Pty Ltd
11 Munro Street, Port Melbourne, Victoria 3207

Copyright © Dawn Richardson-Hyde 1995
First Published 1995

National Library of Australia
Cataloguing-in-publication data:

Richardson-Hyde, Dawna.

Ceramics.

Bibliography.
Includes index.
ISBN 0 85091 625 9.

1. Ceramics. 2. Pottery craft. I. Title. (Series: Lothian Australian craft series).

738

Cover design by Adrian Saunders
Colour photographs by Bill Thomas
Typeset in Garamond by Mackenzies Typesetting, Melbourne
Printed by SNP Printing Pte Ltd, Singapore

WARNING:

Ceramics is a perfectly safe craft if handled correctly. However, many materials it involves are toxic in certain states. Where relevant in the text, icons have been used to advise caution. For further information on toxicity and on health and safety issues, see pages 6, 7, 11 and 12.

Contents

Introduction

Through the projects in this book I would like to encourage you to explore and develop your creativity. Clay is a wonderful medium which can be transformed into a multitude of forms when it is soft. When it is partially dry you can carve it or cut out slabs to construct boxes, cylinders and many 'architectural' forms. Fully dried clay can be sanded and decorated with slip or underglaze.

Simple Ceramics is designed to introduce readers to the art of working with clay. It can also be used by teachers and parents working with children in the field. Hopefully, the information is presented in such a way that beginners can work freely and directly without fear of failure and others with some experience will be able to advance their skills.

The book is divided into three sections. The first contains general information on the materials, tools, equipment and facilities you will need in order to take up simple ceramics. The second details methods and processes commonly used. You would be wise to read the first two sections thoroughly before embarking on the last part of the book—projects for the kitchen and garden.

The projects, which range from simple spoon rests to an extravagant bird bath, are grouped roughly according to skill level. Some span a broad range of skills. Often the simpler projects are useful as a decorating exercise for those with more advanced skills.

The skill levels of the projects are denoted by the following icons:

Ⓒ Children

Ⓢ Children supervised by adults

Ⓑ Beginners

Ⓘ Intermediate

Ⓐ Advanced.

The ultimate challenge, no matter what your degree of expertise, is to make discoveries for yourself. In this book I hope to inspire and challenge, to share my knowledge, and to impart my love of clay and all that it encompasses.

Materials, Equipment and Facilities

Approaches to ceramics (or potting) vary along with the personality and intentions of each person who chooses this craft as their medium of self-expression. They include working on the potter's wheel, hand-building, painting with glaze and modelling, to create a variety of sculptural, decorative and/or functional works. Whatever their approach, all ceramicists (or potters) have one thing in common: they all work with clay.

Working with Clay

Clay is one of the most exciting natural materials on earth. When it is soft it can be shaped in a great variety of ways; once it is fired in a kiln it becomes hard and stone-like. Dry clay can be soaked in water to be brought back to its 'plastic' state; but when glazed and fired in a kiln, it will hold liquids and can be used to cook food in.

Clay exists in abundance, is relatively cheap and can be made into many different ceramic products—from clay tiles and pipes to toilets, bricks, dinnerware, floor tiles and electric insulators. Even parts of the nose cone on spacecraft are made out of clay fired at very high temperatures.

Clay has many colours, due to minerals present in the clay body. In liquid form it can be cast into plaster moulds, or made into a '*slip*' and painted onto pots for decoration or to vary the colour of the pot. Clay with a soft, plastic consistency can be 'thrown' on the potter's wheel, rolled into slabs and coils for hand-building, laid into or on top of plaster moulds, or stamped out as tiles.

When clay is partially dry it can be cut into accurate shapes and joined together to create forms that could not be made on the potter's wheel. Once completely dry, it can be carved, scraped and sanded to achieve further refinement.

Types of Clay

There are many different types of clay, each with varying properties. Rarely can clay be dug from the ground ready to use. Most often it has to be blended with other materials such as sand, feldspars, grog or quartz to form a clay body with suitable colour, texture, workability, shrinkage, and firing temperature for the job at hand.

The three most commonly used clays are:

Earthenware clay

These low-firing clays are usually porous and must be glazed if they are to contain liquids and be able to be cleaned. The firing range for these clays is between 750ºC and 1200ºC. Red earthenware (commonly known as terracotta) clay, is often used for plant pots, roofing tiles and drain pipes. White earthenware is another type of low-fire clay, which is used for brightly decorated and glazed functional ware and tiles.

Stoneware clay

These clays mature to a dense, non-porous body at temperatures between 1200ºC and 1300ºC. Often used by studio potters for producing dinnerware and other functional items, stoneware bodies contain clays and non-plastic additions to improve workability and reduce drying and firing problems. A variety of stoneware clays can be mixed together to form clay bodies with particular properties. Often grey, buff or brown in colour, stoneware can have a variety of textures. Stoneware clay is relatively free from iron compounds and the alkaline fluxes that characterise low-fire clays.

Porcelain clay

This is the highest firing of clays. Due to its large particle size, it is less plastic than stoneware or earthenware clay. Once fired to maturing temperatures of between 1280ºC and 1400ºC it is extremely hard and non-porous. Thin-walled porcelain which is high-fired is *translucent* and often pure white. While its low plasticity (see page 6) can limit the forms to which it is suited, its whiteness and translucency are highly valued, giving purity and elegance to the work.

The clay required for projects in this book is specified at the beginning of each project. Suppliers are listed on page 61.

Characteristics of Clay

A 'good' clay is one that will enable the maker to do what they intend with the material easily and economically. As each person's potting needs may differ, so may the qualities of the clay required.

The clay body must at least be able to be formed into the required shape without cracking, sagging or falling apart. The standard of workability required for clay to be thrown on a potter's wheel differs from that for clay to be used for hand-building, sculptural work or tiles.

For anyone working with clay, the operative properties are its plasticity, texture, green strength, maturing temperature and firing range.

Plasticity

When clay is responsive and easy to manipulate without cracking, it is referred to as having a 'plastic' quality. Some clays are more plastic than others. The smaller the particle size, the more plastic the clay; and often, the greater the shrinkage during drying and firing. Ball clay is very plastic, whereas kaolin is low in plasticity.

Texture

A clay body is made up of a variety of materials of differing particle size. Clays such as ball clay and porcelain have very fine, smooth textures which allow a finely finished surface but can cause more shrinkage during drying and firing. Coarser clays produce a rougher, more varied surface, giving a natural appearance and allowing greater strength and workability. They present fewer shrinkage problems during drying and firing. The texture of a clay body can be altered from fine to coarse by the addition of *grog*, silica, feldspar or shale, making it ideal for larger work, sculpture and hand-building.

Green strength

This refers to the strength of dry clay before firing. It is essential that a clay have enough green strength to allow reasonable handling of pieces during drying and storage before firing.

Maturing temperature and firing range

The maturing temperature of a given clay represents the stage at which, due to the factors of time and temperature, *vitrification* of the clay body occurs. This is the point at which the clay has acquired the density and hardness necessary for its intended use. The maturing temperature is normally stated on the bag in which the clay is sold or on a separate sheet giving technical information about the clay.

The firing range is the temperature spread over which the clay may reasonably be fired to obtain maturity. Earthenware clays have a much narrower firing range than stoneware or porcelain. Care must be taken not to fire clay past its maturing point, otherwise it will warp, slump or stick to the kiln shelf.

Toxicity

In its plastic state clay is not harmful to work with. However, when dry, care must be taken to avoid inhaling clay dust. This dust contains silica, which accumulates in the lungs when breathed in over a period of time. Before embarking on any ceramics projects pay careful attention to the health and safety sections in this book (pages 11, 12–13). Also note the icons used throughout the text to advise caution.

!
CAUTION

Preparation

The beauty of clay is that, with proper treatment, discarded, dried out clay can be re-used. In fact, clay improves with age! Your initial supply of clay must be purchased, in bags in its plastic state, but all those dried out bits and pieces left over from your work, and pots that crack in the drying out stage can be recycled. Prepare dried out clay in the following way:

- Wearing a mask and working outdoors so as to avoid inhaling the dust (silica), place the clay between two layers of newspaper and crush it by pounding with a rubber mallet.
- *Slake* it into a bin one-third full of water, and mix it into a *slurry*, which you can then dry to plastic state once again for re-use. A little vinegar added to the water in which the clay is slaking will aid plasticity.
- To dry the slurry, spread it on a plaster bat, cement sheeting, or wooden frames with canvas stretched over them; excess moisture will be drawn out of the clay, advancing it to its plastic state.
- Finally, you *wedge* the clay in order to create a homogeneous body free from lumps or air pockets. (See *Wedging*, page 16) Wedging is always repeated just before using the clay.

Storage

Once you have prepared and wedged the clay, wrap it tightly in plastic to retain moisture and prevent drying. Clay bought pre-prepared in plastic bags should be checked before storage to ensure that it is tightly sealed and there are no holes in the bags. Plastic garbage bins with wire-clipped lids are effective for storing bags of recycled clay. Always reseal the plastic bag—there is nothing more frustrating than trying to work with hard clay.

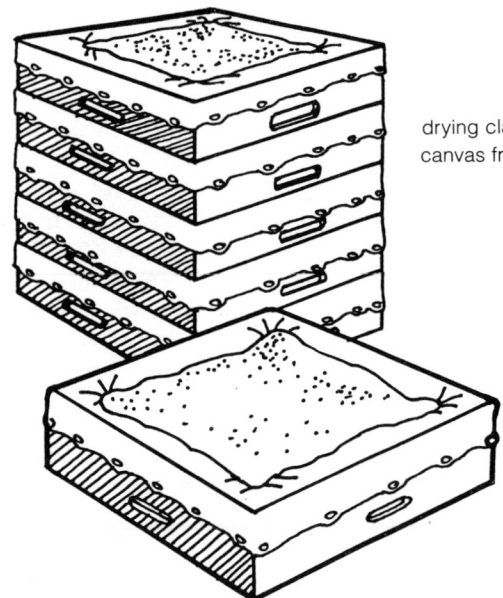

drying clay on canvas frames

Working with Glaze

What is Glaze?

Glaze is glass made up of a selection of raw materials which have been collected in rock form, ground into fine powders and combined. When applied to a clay surface and fired in a kiln, these materials melt together to produce a glaze.

Glaze results can vary greatly depending on three factors:

- the type and colour of the clay body underneath the glaze
- the temperature the glaze is fired to
- the kiln atmosphere—oxidation or reduction (see page 15).

Why Do We Glaze?

There are two main reasons for glazing a piece of work. One is to give it colour, texture, or any of a large choice of decorative effects. The other is to make the piece waterproof and thus able to contain liquids. This is important when making functional ware since a smooth, faultless glaze provides a hygienic covering.

Handy Tips

While working with glaze can be the most exciting aspect of ceramics, it can also be the most problematical. You would therefore be wise to follow a few handy tips.

- Develop a good understanding of the raw materials and the part they play in glaze formulation.
- Be thorough in your approach to testing. Keep accurate records of the results of glaze tests. This must include proper labelling and numbering of tests, thorough recording of results in a variety of firings, and an inquiring attitude towards the development of new recipes. To prevent disasters and retain your sanity always make tests before committing a full kiln load of work to a new glaze recipe.
- Learn to read a glaze recipe and mix a glaze from a percentage recipe. Learn how to increase the quantity of a recipe.
- Understand how to adjust raw glaze materials to change the character or quality of a glaze, or alter the maturing temperature, and be able to substitute raw materials in order to achieve similar qualities using available materials (in other words, improvise).
- Develop an understanding of glaze faults and how they might be corrected.

- Experience and experiment with the effects of different glazes in combination.
- Gain an understanding of appropriate thicknesses and proper techniques for application.

Toxicity

A large number of glaze materials are toxic in their raw state and therefore need to be handled using proper protection—gloves and a mask—in a clean, well-ventilated work area with an efficient extractor fan.

Maturing Temperatures

Glazes are formulated to mature at a variety of temperatures. High-fire glazes will not mature at lower temperatures, and low-fire glazes will be overfired if taken to high (stoneware) temperatures. The maturing temperature of the glaze is linked to that of the clay. Some clays have a broad firing range and are suitable for earhenware and stoneware glaze firings.

Clay type	Firing range	Glaze classification
Raku	900–1060ºC	Low-fire glazes
Earthenware	1020–1160ºC	
Earthenware and stoneware	1160–1220ºC	Mid-fire glazes
Stoneware and porcelain	1260–1450ºC	High-fire glazes

Buying and Using Prepared Glaze

Ceramics suppliers offer a large range of prepared glazes of all colours, finishes and temperature ranges. Some glazes come in jars ready for painting onto your work. Pre-mixed glazes in plastic containers of one litre or more are available for dipping, pouring or spraying onto your work. If you prefer to buy bags of pre-mixed dry glaze materials all you need do is add water, mix and sieve before applying to your work. For people with limited time to make glaze, and students not yet confident in glaze preparation who wish to have a reliable result, these are useful options. The ultimate limitations when you wish to glaze larger quantities of work will be their cost, and predictability!

Mixing Your Own Glazes

When you wish to make the transition to preparing, testing and using glazes from the seemingly unlimited recipes offered in glaze books, or concocting your own variations, you will need to stock your studio with some basic glaze-making materials. Your cue to purchasing what you require will come from the recipes you wish to test for potential use. Before 'buying out the shop' you would be wise to ask yourself the following questions:

- Which temperature range do I wish to explore? This may be determined by the type of kiln you have access to, and its maximum heating capacity.
- Do I wish to work with an electric kiln (oxidation—see page 15), a gas kiln (reduction—see page 15), raku firing, wood or salt-firing?
- What type of work do I wish to produce? Functional, decorative, sculptural work, salt-glazed, terracotta, raku-fired, wood-fired? All require different glaze considerations.
- What are my limitations? Space? Money? Time? Ability and technical knowledge?

Understanding Glaze Recipes

Glaze recipes usually specify the type of glaze (stoneware or earthenware), the finish (matt, satin, shiny, dry), the degree of opacity (clear, opaque or translucent), the maturing temperature or temperature the glaze is fired to (for example, 1250ºC or by cone 6), and the kiln atmosphere (either oxidation, or reduction).

The ingredients in most glaze recipes are listed as a percentage of total weight, usually in descending order. For example:

Potash feldspar	50.0 (%)
Ball clay	20.0
Whiting	20.0
Magnesium carbonate (light)	10.0

The list of ingredients forms the *base glaze* recipe. This recipe be altered to make the glaze more translucent or opaque, vary its firing temperature or make it shiny or matt. Stains and oxides can be added to the base glaze in order to change its colour. Any added colourants are always listed in addition to the base glaze.

Weighing and mixing

- Have the recipe you wish to make on a card in front of you with the required amounts worked out in grams.
- Wear a mask to prevent inhalation of airborne glaze dust, and if handling a toxic material, wear plastic gloves. Work outside or in an area with an extractor fan.
- Have ready a plastic glaze container with a lid into which you can put materials as they are weighed.
- Weigh materials in the order given, ticking off each material on the list as you place it in the plastic container. Accurate weighing is imperative.

- When all dry materials are in the container, add a small amount of water to allow dry materials to soak down, then add small amounts of water and mix using an electric drill with a paint-mixing bit. The consistency of the glaze should be like thickened cream. When you dip your dry finger in the mix it should coat your finger, with the outline of your fingernail visible through the coating.
- Ensure that any lumps are dissolved into the mix.
- Sieve through a 120-mesh sieve (twice preferably) to ensure a smooth consistency.
- Place your mixture in a glaze storage container and label the top and side for easy identification. Marking the glaze name, recipe number and firing temperature will provide the required information at a glance, while attaching a fired test sample of the glaze is ideal.

Note: It is a good idea to mix the glaze up a few days before use to allow the glaze to settle and eliminate the bubbles that occur during mixing.

Increasing quantities

Glaze materials are weighed in dry powder form on a triple beam balance scale calibrated in grams and kilograms. Since most glaze batch recipes total 100 (%) it is simple to increase the quantity of a recipe proportionally, as shown in the table.

	100 g	500 g	1000 g
Potash feldspar	50.0	250.0	500.0
Ball clay	20.0	100.0	200.0
Whiting	20.0	100.0	200.0
Magnesium carbonate light	10.0 = 100	50.0 = 500	100.0 = 1000
Add: Iron oxide	5.0	25.0	50.0
Cobalt	.5	2.5	5.0

Note:
- 100 g batches of glaze are a useful amount for testing.
- 500–2000 g batches are useful quantities for glazing your work.

Storing Mixed Glazes

Most glazes will store indefinitely in plastic buckets with tightly fitting lids. Because glazes settle to varying degrees, the glaze will require stirring or re-sieving before use to return it to an ideal consistency for glazing. A drop of vinegar in the glaze will help prevent settling, as will inclusion of bentonite in the glaze recipe.

Working with Plaster

Plaster provides valuable support to working with clay. A naturally occurring material, it was first mined commercially near Paris—hence the name 'plaster of Paris'. When mixed with water, plaster recombines to form a soft, porous stone. The capacity of plaster to reproduce in great detail the form and surface texture of an object onto which it is poured and allowed to set makes it useful for replicating objects in clay.

Plaster comes in variety of grades, from the coarse builder's plaster to a very fine grained, dense dental plaster. Potter's plaster, ideal for working in clay, is available from ceramics suppliers. Quick-setting plaster is also suitable and may be obtained at hardware or building supply shops, usually more cheaply than potter's plaster.

When properly mixed with water and allowed to harden, plaster is a homogeneous material—that is, it has no grain or lumps. In its early stages before setting, plaster has the consistency of thickened cream, and can be *poured*. It later enters a plastic state during, which it can be worked with templates and tools. At this stage it can be manipulated to build up models over a framework, or *turned* on a lathe or on a potter's wheel to create forms for casting or press-moulding. Once dry, plaster may be *sanded* with tool called a surform or *carved* to create detailed low-relief.

Plaster will not shrink when set, which makes it easy to use for reproduction purposes. It is a relatively inexpensive material; potters use and discard large amounts of plaster in their day-to-day work.

In ceramics, plaster can be used for:
- press moulds and drape moulds (see page 19)
- wedging boards (see page 12)
- plaster bats to dry liquid clay on (see page 6)
- carved stamps or tiles for impressing into clay
- casting into sand to create textured surfaces on which clay slabs can be formed.

General Tips

- Once opened, plaster has a limited storage life. It is best bought as needed rather than stored indefinitely in large amounts. Always store your plaster in an airtight container, as it absorbs moisture.
- Plaster and clay don't mix—if plaster is allowed to get into clay it will cause the clay to split open or bloat when fired in the kiln.
- If heated to 150ºC or above, plaster will become 'deadburnt'—that is, weak and powdery—so it is best not to force-dry your moulds in an oven or kiln.
- Plaster needs to be worked with quickly, before it hardens. The trick is to plan ahead. Decide exactly what you want to do with it, and prepare your workspace and items to be moulded so that everything is ready before you mix up the plaster.

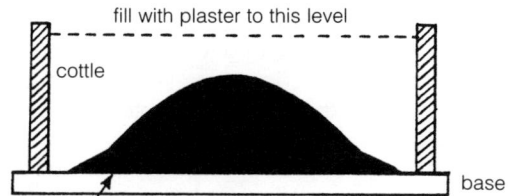

fill with plaster to this level

cottle

base

this form (either an original piece or a clay model you have made) should be coated with a releasing agent

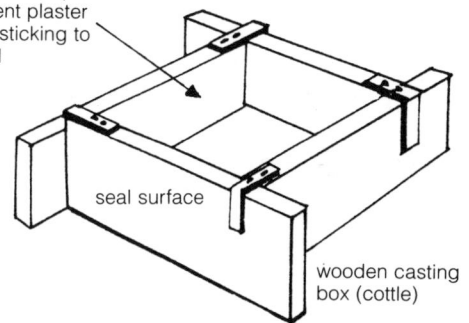

use soft soap to prevent plaster from sticking to wood

seal surface

wooden casting box (cottle)

- Plaster will clog drains. Allow unwanted plaster to harden, then discard it, rather than pouring it down the sink in liquid form. Plastic buckets, basins, ice-cream containers, etc. are ideal for collecting unwanted plaster—when it dries it will just pop out.
- Old plaster will contaminate a new mix. Make sure all containers for mixing plaster are thoroughly clean before mixing a new batch.
- Plaster must be mixed with **water**—not meths, turps or oil.
- Always add plaster to water—never the other way around.
- Because plaster is a soft, brittle material when dry, moulds must be handled with care.
- Plaster sticks to plaster—handy if you want to patch, but not so if you don't want your plaster to stick to the form you are moulding. A releasing agent such as clay slip or soft soap can be painted onto the form to be cast to prevent this.
- Several factors affect the time taken for plaster to set:
  - water to plaster ratio—denser mixes set more quickly
  - temperature of the water—hot water speeds up setting
  - mixing energy—the faster you mix the plaster, the faster it sets. Slow, gentle mixing works best, and minimises bubbles.

    Additions of *alum* and *salt* increase the speed of the set. *Alcohol* and *size* added to the mix will retard the set.

Preparation

Always prepare your plaster in a work area separate from your pottery production area, or ensure that work tables are covered with discardable plastic. Be very tidy in mixing and clean-up.

- Before mixing up the plaster prepare your models for pouring—that is, surround them with a *cottle* of plastic or clay to contain the plaster, and paint a separator, or releasing agent (clay slip, soft soap), onto the surface of the piece to be moulded.
- Collect small forms or pie dishes into which spare plaster can be poured to make portable bats or drape moulds.
- Have a large container of water handy—large plastic buckets are ideal—to wash out the mixing container. Remember: never wash plaster down the sink as it will settle, set and block the pipes.

Mixing and Casting

For mixing you will need the following items:

- scoop, or ice-cream or margarine container, to scoop the powder from the bag (don't get this wet)
- bucket to mix the plaster in
- garbage bin containing water to clean mixing buckets, etc.
- plastic garbage bin lined with a plastic bag to take excess plaster
- scales to weigh the plaster.

For casting you will need:

- a base board to make your model on—this should be 10 cm bigger than the model all the way around; masonite, glass or plastic work well
- clay to make the model—a fine ungrogged clay will give the best surface; once you have modelled this clay keep it separate and use it only for plaster
- cottles to contain the fluid plaster when it is poured—these can be made of linoleum, plastic or wooden frames (boards) coated with lacquer; plaster is heavy when wet—make sure your cottles are strong enough to contain it
- additional tools to cut, clean up or shape the hardened plaster, i.e. hacksaw blade, surforms, files, rasps, etc.
- metal scrapers, steel wool, fine sandpaper for finishing the dry plaster surfaces.

To mix plaster:

1 Estimate the volume to be filled with plaster.
- Allow an extra 20%—better to have too much than not enough!
- Once the volume is established, multiply by 5 and divide by 7. This gives the volume of water required.

   For example, to cast a form which will hold about 1 litre of plaster (1000 ml):

- add 20% = 1200
- multiply by 5 = 6000
- divide by 7 = 857.1

   Thus, the volume of water required is 857.1 ml to the volume of dry plaster (1200 g).

2 Measure into a plastic bucket the required volume of water and weigh out the required amount of plaster.

3 Slowly sift the plaster into the water. When the mix is nearly right, the plaster should sit on the surface and sink slowly.

4 Allow plaster to *slake* undisturbed for one minute.

5 Stir the plaster by immersing your arm in it and gently moving your hand. Discard any hard lumps. Gradually the mix will lose its watery consistency and begin to feel like thick cream.

6 Tap the sides of the container to encourage any air bubbles to rise to the surface. Skim these off, and prepare to pour the mix. Work carefully and quickly—as soon as dry powdered plaster is added to water, an irreversible action begins which ends in crystallisation and hardening of the mix.

7 As soon as you have finished mixing, pour the plaster into your mould, agitating the mould to obtain good coverage of the surface detail and to allow trapped air bubbles to rise to the surface.

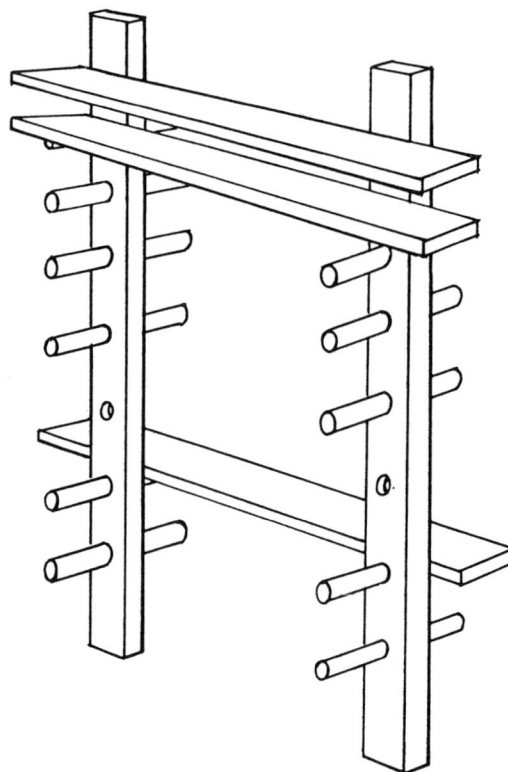

Movable storage shelves

Planning a Work Space

A ceramics studio can be a corner of a room; a garage or a tin shed in the back garden; or a purpose-built retreat. I have worked in the spare bedroom of an apartment, lining the walls and carpet with plastic sheeting, and more recently in a compact but well-organised space built specially as a clay studio.

If you have recently discovered working with clay you may wish to experiment for a while before making the longer term commitment of setting up a permanent studio. In doing so, bear in mind that even a temporary work space must address a number of key issues.

Health and Safety

If you plan to work in a kitchen or another room of your home, you must remember that clay dust and some glaze materials are toxic. Dry clay should be scraped or sanded out of doors, and glaze should be handled (weighed, mixed and applied) outside or in a well-ventilated area. Never spray glaze in an enclosed area without an extractor fan to remove the glaze particles from the air. Always wear a mask when spraying glaze.

You should never work with ceramics where food is being prepared or eaten.

Storage of Materials

Materials should be stored in an outside shed or a carport, rather than inside the home. Lidded plastic containers for clay and glazes are effective receptacles. Make sure you clearly label glaze materials, using a waterproof felt marker, on both the top and side of the container. Clearly identify any toxic materials.

To stop your ceramic pieces drying out during the making process, wrap them in light plastic (dry-cleaning bags work well) and store them in a cupboard with doors for protection. Work that is drying or has been dried ready for firing should preferably be stored in a shed or a covered area outside the home to minimise clay dust.

Disposal of Waste

!
CAUTION

Toxic materials must be disposed of carefully—not thrown down the sink! Local councils will often collect these for special disposal. I scrape any glaze material into a bucket, allow it to settle, syphon off the water and allow the remaining substances to dry for special disposal. Developing good work practices will ensure a safe working environment and prevent pollution of our natural environment.

Cleanliness

Glazing pots by pouring, painting or dipping can be a messy job, and needs special care, particularly if you are set up in a temporary location. Plastic sheeting makes clean-up of splashes and spills easier.

A Portable Work Surface

A temporary working surface can be created by placing on an existing table a canvas-covered work board (13 mm chipboard works well) measuring up to one metre square. The canvas is easily sponged clean and removed when work is complete. Canvas provides a non-stick surface suitable for wedging clay and rolling slabs or coils on. Smaller pieces of plasterboard or cement sheeting are useful to extract moisture from clay slabs, allowing them to 'set up' before construction begins. Craftboard, a very fine grained chipboard, also works well.

A Permanent Work Space

If you do graduate to a permanent work space you will find it helpful to designate particular areas for specific tasks—for example, preparing clay, making pieces, storing work at various stages of completion, preparing glazes, applying glazes, and so on.

Space limitations and finances will ultimately determine the working layout of your studio, but some essential facilities, all of which you can build yourself, are described below.

A drying cupboard

You can make a drying cupboard, used to prevent work from drying out too quickly, by lining the opening of a portable closet with plastic sheeting, or by surrounding an open wooden shelving system with overlapping layers of plastic hung vertically from the top of the shelves to enclose the space. This allows unwrapped work to dry slowly.

Movable storage shelves

There are many approaches to shelving but one I have found most adaptable consists of 4 cm x 10 cm pine uprights drilled at 25 cm intervals with holes 2.5 cm in diameter. Two of these uprights, one on either side about 80 cm apart, are wedged between the floor and ceiling and lengths of wooden dowel are placed into the holes. Boards approximately 15 cm wide x 1 metre long can then be placed on the dowels at varying heights according to the demands of the work. You can easily lift the boards off the dowels and carry them to another area of the studio, without having to move individual pieces of work. This system works well for free-standing shelves dividing open areas of the work space. You can create additional shelving on either side of the uprights by doubling the length of the dowels, pushing them through the holes so that half the length is on either side of the post, and placing boards on either side.

A work table or bench

A workbench with access on all four sides is ideal for a ceramicist. Important factors are the sturdiness and weight of the table; the heavier the better, in order to prevent movement when you roll large slabs of clay.

The surface should be easy to wash and non-stick. Chipboard tends to become rough with too much washing unless it is sealed. A plastic-laminated wood can work well providing it has non-stick areas to roll slabs and wedge on. Craftwood or smooth cement sheeting make excellent work surfaces. Storage space underneath the table will increase the functional use of space in your studio.

A wedging table

Wedging can be done on any non-stick sturdy surface. For logistical reasons your wedging table should ideally be near your clay preparation and storage area. A wooden frame with a base, filled with plaster of Paris and covered in canvas makes a suitable wedging table. Sturdy legs and a cutting wire attached are essential for successful wedging of clay.

The height of your table should be about level with your forearms when you hold these parallel to the surface. This is important because you need to use the weight of your entire body to wedge, rather than relying on strong arms and shoulders.

Canvas-covered work boards

A selection of 15 mm thick chipboard covered in canvas and varying in size, or masonite that has been coated with Estapol to seal the surface, make excellent working surfaces (known as 'bats') for various tasks. The portability of such bats means that work need not be disturbed while in progress but may be moved and stored later. Canvas provides a non-stick surface, while masonite is easier to clean.

A water source

While a sink with running water is useful in the studio, it is not a necessity. Large plastic buckets of water can be brought into the studio for mixing glaze, clean-up, etc.

A spray booth

If you are planning to spray glaze onto your work you must have a contained area with a strong extraction fan to filter and remove glaze vapour from your studio. Spray booths can be constructed from sheet metal, or are available commercially. They should be located in your glaze preparation area and have the capacity to be closed off when not in use.

Bats for recycling clay

Liquid clay, or slurry, which must be partially dried before being wedged, requires a place to set up. A system of wood frames stacked one on top of another with canvas draped horizontally in between, which will allow air to filter through, is one such facility. Another is plaster bats, which suck moisture out of the clay. Since the latter are not stackable, availability of space will decide which option is best for you.

Health and Safety in a Permanent Studio

Long-term, it is preferable to work in an area that is not a living space for you or your family. Accumulated dusts can cause respiratory problems over time, particularly in young children, and the adverse effects of toxic chemicals are well known. Some of the health and safety considerations listed below are common sense, others require installation of equipment.

- Regular studio clean-up is a common sense approach to minimising dust hazards. By damp-mopping floors, sponging shelves and work surfaces, and cleaning tools after use you can prevent build-up of dust in the studio.
- Thorough vacuuming is necessary, and preferable to sweeping with a broom. Sweeping tends to disperse clay dust into the air, which is then breathed in, whereas regular vacuuming takes away the dust and damp-mopping damps it down.
- Adequate lighting, particularly where you are doing detailed work, will prevent eyestrain and headaches.
- Proper ventilation, including a good extractor fan, is essential, particularly in a glaze preparation area where dry chemicals are being weighed and mixed.
- Storage of materials should be as described on pages 6 and 8. Buckets should be stored where they can be easily reached. Save back problems: store heavy materials such as bags of clay and heavy glaze buckets on waist-high shelves. Garbage bins containing reclaimed clay should be stored on wooden bases with wheels to make them portable.
- A dust mask should be worn when mixing dry materials such as glaze chemicals or dried up clay for slip, and when sanding, scraping or carving dry clay, to prevent inhalation of particles.
- Eye protection, in the form of goggles is important when chipping or grinding glaze from bottoms of pots or kiln shelves.
- Rubber gloves should be worn for mixing glazes that contain toxic chemicals.
- All toxic materials must be identified clearly.

CAUTION

• Your kiln should be located in an area separate from your regular working space, with adequate ventilation, as kilns give off fumes during the early stages of firing. Proper extractor fans or a well-ventilated kiln shed are absolutely necessary for gas kilns, in particular.
• Eating and drinking are best avoided while you are working. Any food or drink brought into the studio might absorb harmful chemicals. If you want to drink or eat, take a break away from your work area.

Tools and Equipment

It is said that a craftsperson is only as good as their tools, but when working with clay your hands are often the best tool you can use! Hands are more sensitive than any inanimate object to the texture, consistency and surface qualities of clay. In addition, simple tools from the kitchen are a good starting point and will serve you well, many of them being able to be adapted to broaden your range of techniques. At the beginning of my potting career some twenty years ago I acquired tools that I still use and regard with great fondness, often remembering the circumstances in which they came into my possession. As you become more involved in working with clay, your tool kit will grow. A fishing tackle box acts as an ideal storage case for tools.

In Table 2 (page 14) I have listed the tools generally required for making the projects in this book, together with their application. While these tools are typically used for hand-built ceramics, many of them can be used to make wheel-thrown pots as well.

In addition to these tools you will find it convenient to have on hand basic studio materials and utensils, such as plastic garbage bins and buckets of varying size, with lids; sheets of plastic to wrap work in; large plastic bowls for pouring glaze into; measuring cups; a variety of plastic jugs; and a sponge mop.

When it comes to texturing clay, many 'found' objects can be used. Buttons, a spring stretched out and pulled through clay to create ridges, 'Afro' combs, a garlic press, toy car wheels, a pasta cutter, nuts and sea shells, twigs, pine cones, seedpods, short lengths of rope rolled on the clay's surface, even a meat tenderiser can all be experimented with.

As far as equipment is concerned, it is advisable to start with only the necessities (see Table 1), and attend to the extras when you are certain you want to continue working with clay, and have the necessary space and funds to do so.

While having a kiln of your own is ideal, it is not absolutely necessary in the beginning. Even long-term, you might choose to own an electric kiln, and 'borrow' a gas kiln, or vice versa, since many projects (including those in this book) require the use of both. Plenty of services exist which will charge by

the cubic foot to fire your work. You could also investigate your local community house or centre and schools, which often have kilns. While these groups may not have a policy of hiring out space, you might be able to negotiate an offer to help with loading and firing the kiln, and perhaps pay a small fee.

Any additional tools and equipment required for the individual projects in this book are listed, as required, at the beginning of each project.

Table 1

Equipment	Application
120-mesh sieve	Used for straining out lumps and sieving slip and glaze to an even consistency; available at ceramic suppliers
Banding wheel	Useful when making coil pots, but are not a necessity; available at ceramic suppliers
Canvas-covered chip-board 15 mm thick x 1 m square or large piece plasterboard	A portable non-stick work surface which can be placed on top of a kitchen table in a temporary workshop situation
Electric drill with a paint-mixing bit	To mix up slip and glazes
Plastic buckets with lids	To store or re-cycle clay, for glaze material storage wet and dry
Slab-rolling guide sticks 2 x 600 mm long x 30 mm wide x 10 mm thick	For rolling even slabs; obtainable at a lumber yard
Triple-beam balance scale	If you wish to weigh out your own glazes rather than rely on pre-mixed ones, you will need accurate scales. These are an expensive item (not necessary when starting), but useful as your involvement grows.

Banding wheel

Table 2

Tools	Application	Tools	Application
Ballpoint pens	Writing in soft clay	Nailbrush	Texturing
Bamboo skewers—short and long	Making holes, scoring, texturing	Nails—large	Making holes in clay
Clay tools—wooden, various (including ribbed)	Modelling and refining detail; dragging	Paddles—wooden, plain and textured	Firming up and consolidating coil forms
Cotton buds	Smearing painted surfaces	Paintbrushes—various sizes	Applying slip and glazes
Crochet hooks	Texturing; for smoothing and texturing in inaccessible joins	Pin tool	Cutting, marking, scoring
Cutting wire	Cutting clay from block	Plastic wrap	Wrapping work, to set up
		Popsicle sticks	Texturing
Dental tools	Carving into leatherhard or dry clay	Rollers—bisqued clay	Decorating, texture
Drill bits—various sizes	Making clean holes		
Face mask	Used while weighing and mixing glazes		
File—metal jeweller's	Smoothing and refining dry clay	Rolling pin—miniature/cake decorating	Rolling small slabs
Forks—plastic or metal	Texturing clay	Rolling pin—plain	Rolling slabs of clay
Gloves—disposable rubber	Weighing and mixing, and applying glazes	Rolling pin—ridged	Texturing clay
Hairdryer or heat gun	Stiffening clay quickly	Ruler—metal	Used as a measuring and cutting guide
Handcream	Moisturising hands	Sandpaper—fine and medium	Smoothing and refining dry clay
Handtowel	Drying hands		
Kidney—metal	Scraping and refining leatherhard or dry clay	Scissors	Cutting
Kidney—rubber	Smoothing clay surface	Scourers—green plastic	Smoothing and refining dry clay
Kidney—wooden	Forming clay	Sgraffito tool	Scratching through slip or into clay (the tool has a sharp metal point)
Knives—clay, kitchen and long-bladed	Cutting clay	Sponges—various textures	Cleaning up clay surfaces and studio; for stamped decoration
Knife—serrated	Roughening clay surface (texture)	Spoons—plastic or metal	Smoothing and burnishing leatherhard clay
Leather pieces	Smoothing edges of clay	Stamps—bisqued clay	Decorating, texture
Looped tool—metal (small)	Hollowing out clay		
		Steel wool	Smoothing and refining dry clay
		Stones—polished	Burnishing
		Toothbrushes—old	Scoring clay slabs to be joined; texturing
Metal extruder—mini	Creating small, uniform coils; for decorating	Trimming tools—metal	Cleaning up; finishing

The Kiln

A kiln is a form of high-temperature oven used to bake clay. This *firing* process makes the shape you have built in soft clay permanent. Kilns draw on a variety of fuels as a heat source. Although the original wood-fired kiln has regained popularity due to the beautiful and varied effects it can produce, most of today's kilns are fired using electricity, or natural or bottled LP gas. Some are fired with oil. Due to practicalities of location and time available, the electric kiln is perhaps the best suited to urban life-styles.

Electric kilns are made of soft firebricks with high insulating capacity. In the bricks are grooves into which high-temperature kanthal elements are fitted. The exterior of the kiln is stainless steel (to prevent rust and corrosion). The smaller, lower-temperature kilns will run off your household electricity supply, but the larger, higher-temperature kilns will require two- or three-phase power. Ask your supplier to show you kilns suited to your facilities, and have a qualified electrician wire your kiln into the power supply.

Gas kilns are available commercially or, with proper understanding and knowledge, you can build your own (see *Further Reading*, page 63). Soft and hard firebrick or fibre are the most common materials used to build these. Bottled LP gas or natural gas and properly specified *venturi* burners correctly plumbed into the kiln provide the fuel source. Gas kilns have the capacity to fire to temperatures of 1300°C, which is ideal for stoneware or porcelain, with the additional advantage of variation in the atmosphere in the kiln (see *Oxidation and reduction*, below).

Oxidation and reduction firings

Firing clay in an atmosphere which has plenty of air (and therefore oxygen) results in oxidation. Electric kilns have an oxidising atmosphere unless a combustible substance (for example, wood) is put in the kiln (not advisable as it will damage kiln elements). Gas, oil and wood kilns can be oxidised by opening air ports to allow more oxygen into the chamber and by increasing primary air.

Firing clay in an atmosphere with inadequate air (oxygen) results in reduction. The atmosphere (usually in a gas, oil or wood kiln) is smoky because the carbon is not being completely burnt. A reduction firing changes the oxides (for example, copper, which fires to green in oxidation, will fire red in reduction). The clay body will also change colour in a reduction firing.

Care and maintenance of your kiln

Your new kiln should come with the manufacturer's information on firing, care and maintenance. If not, following a few simple steps will ensure long life and safe operation of this crucial piece of equipment.

After a few firings, vacuum your kiln (wear a mask) to remove bits of fired debris from the inside. Bits of clay commonly lodge in the elements, shortening their operating life. To check that elements haven't bulged out of their groove or broken, turn the kiln to high, leave for fifteen minutes, then open it. All the elements should be at red heat—any that are not may be broken or worn out. If elements are bulged out of their groove, turn off power and, using a piece of wood, gently push the hot element back into its groove.

Check gas burners regularly to ensure that bits of debris haven't fallen inside blocking the burner orifice.

Kiln shelves should be dusted off and checked for glaze spills after each firing. If spills have occurred, grind the shelf down to remove the glaze, and paint a new kiln wash (see page 60) onto the shelf.

Check that the roof of the kiln is intact. Debris from a cracked kiln roof may drop onto fired pots, ruining them. If cracks occur in the insulating firebrick, you can fill them with a kiln cement.

Take care in handling the pyrometer, which is a very delicate instrument. If the pyrometer is not reading correctly, the weld inside the probe could be broken. Make sure the case covering the wires does not get knocked or broken. Replacements of the probe case can be obtained but if the probe inside is broken, the entire device will require replacing—expense that can be avoided with a little extra care!

If you have an electric kiln make sure the master switch (at the plug outlet), as well as all the switches on the kiln, are in the off position, so that the kiln cannot be turned on accidentally.

! CAUTION

Gas kiln burners and pilots must be left in the off position so that seepage does not occur. Always leave the gas kiln door slightly ajar when not in use and when lighting the kiln's burners, to ensure that gas has not leaked and accumulated inside the kiln.

As kilns are expensive, it is advisable to work with clay for a period of time, using different types of kilns, before deciding whether to purchase or build, and to investigate your options thoroughly before deciding which type and size will best suit your needs. Second-hand kilns can be obtained through newspaper advertisements, pottery groups or potters' magazines. There are also many commercial suppliers of new electric and gas kilns (see page 61) if you are prepared to spend more money.

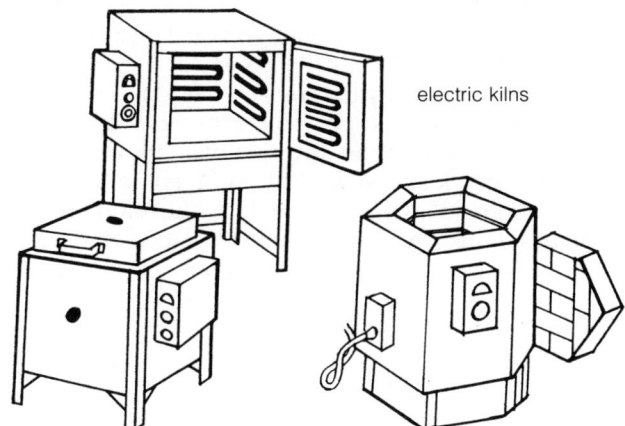

electric kilns

Techniques

Basic Forming Techniques

Wedging

Whether you are using new clay directly from a bag or reclaimed clay, you must wedge all clay before use. Instructions for all projects in this book assume that you have wedged your clay first.

Wedging eliminates air bubbles and gives the clay a smooth, homogeneous consistency. It is best to start with soft clay, as wedging tends to dry clay out, making it difficult and unpleasant to work with.

There are several ways to wedge. To use the 'cut and slam' method, cut a lump of clay in half with the cutting wire attached to your wedging board table (see page 12). Slam the two halves of clay down on top of one another on the table, then turn the clay on its side and repeat the action. Do this until all the clay is of even texture and no bubbles appear when the clay is cut.

The most common method of wedging is to knead the clay, similar to kneading bread. This method is effective and easy to learn with a bit of practice:

- Use a lump of clay of a size that you feel capable of controlling. Until you have mastered the technique and have had lots of practice, you will find it easier to wedge small lumps.
- Start with a rounded lump of clay (Photo 1).
- Stand in front of the wedging table with your back leg straight and your front leg bent. Rock back and forth onto your front leg, keeping your back leg and your back straight. This places less stress on your back and allows you to use the weight of your entire body to work the clay.
- With the heel of each hand, gently push the lump of clay forward (Photo 2).
- Using your fingertips, lift the clay towards you from the back of the lump. As you do so, pat the sides of the lump in—this will keep the clay round and compact, and prevent the sides from splaying out (Photo 3).
- Push the lump of clay forward again with the heels of your hands (Photo 4).

Wedging has a rhythm: push away, lift towards you, pat the sides in, push, pull, pat—and repeat! Don't push too hard on the clay or it will end up being flat: a light, quick action works best. A 'spine' will form in the centre of the lump, in fact, the lump will look like a ramshead or a monkey's face—names often given to this type of wedging (Photo 5).

Photo 1

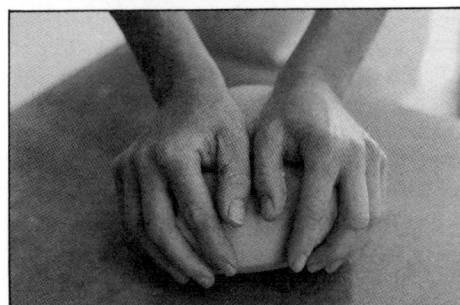

Photo 2

Photo 3

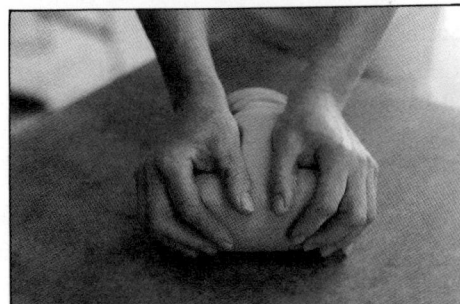

Photo 4

Photo 5

The kitchen becomes a place of creativity and the tasks of preparing and serving food made more enjoyable with the use of the objects pictured here. Clear-glazed black and white spoon rests, spice containers, decorative spoons and the commemorative platter entitled 'Chris catches his first fish' are both practical and unique additions that any cook would enjoy. The delicate pinched cups using porcelain clay coloured black and layered with white porcelain are sure to complement a fine liqueur.

This zany, expressive birdbath will give any garden colour and character. The pieces are made separately, and threaded on to a metal rod. You can fill the birdbath bowl with water, then sit back and watch the birds enjoy their luxury bathing facility.

INSET: A cat sleeps peacefully stretched around the rim of this terracotta wall planter. The inside of the planter is glazed brilliant turquoise, setting off the plants. Drainage holes are located underneath the planter to avoid waterlogging the plants.

Pinching

Pinching is the most direct method of working with clay to make a pot. While also appearing to be the simplest method, the technique requires a quiet, concentrated approach. Although the pinch method is often overlooked, very beautiful and sensitive forms can be achieved.

- Sit on a chair, both hands resting in your lap, with a ball of soft clay the size of a mandarin orange nestled loosely between your fingertips. (If you have long fingernails they will need to be cut or they will continually gouge into the clay.)
- Begin by pushing your right thumb into the centre of the ball of clay until it is 10–15 mm (approximately) from the bottom. With your thumb inside, gently turn the ball of clay while pressing the hole you have made until it gets larger. The fingers on both hands work to support the walls from the outside as you continually turn the pot, pushing from the inside with your thumb to enlarge the hole and keeping the walls even on all sides.
- When the hole is large enough, place both thumbs inside and continue pinching and turning, supporting the outside walls with your fingers.

With concentration you will learn to control the forms you are making, creating even walls and rounded forms. If the sides of the pot start to splay out too much, you can bring them in to a rounded form by using the forefinger and thumb on both hands to pinch and tuck gently.

Don't worry if the rims of your work are slightly uneven—as the pot firms up you may trim the rims with a sharp knife or scissors. It is useful to have a variety of small bowl forms around the studio to support pinched forms as they are being made. These forms, known as 'pukis', can be made out of clay, then bisqued (see page 19).

The walls of your pot can be made quite thin with the pinching method, and if you do not wish to keep the texture made by the pinching, it may be scraped or sanded off when the piece is dry. If you work on a few pieces at the same time, one can be stiffening up while you work on the next one. Rest the stiffening pieces in cups or bowls so as not to flatten the bottoms—wrap the rims in plastic so they don't dry out and you can continue to refine the forms.

Many forms can be created using this method— rounded enclosed forms, outstretched-bowls, forms resembling nature are all possible with practice.

Clay Slabs

To roll the slabs:

- Working on a canvas-covered board or a non-stick, slightly absorbent surface (see page 12), pat wedged clay flat to about 20 mm thick, or slam it down on the work table at a 45° angle to stretch it.
- Place the clay in the centre of two slab-rolling guide sticks. Using a rolling pin, flatten the clay to the thickness of the sticks (10 mm) by allowing the ends of the rolling pin to rest on the guide sticks and pushing the clay gently. The required thickness of your slab (5–15 mm) depends on the size of your project (big pieces require thick slabs for structural stability). To thin slabs further, remove the guide sticks and roll evenly. Note that thin slabs tend to warp and slump if overfired.
- To avoid sticking, dust the rolling pin with some flour or dry clay.
- Gently lift the slab onto a piece of plasterboard or cement sheeting to firm up. (Note: soft clay distorts when cut. The firmer the clay slab, the easier it is to cut a shape that is true.)
- Dry slowly to prevent warping and cracking.

Templates

Templates are the pattern guides for the slab form you wish to build. These are generally cut from cardboard, light or heavy depending on how many times you need to use them. Using templates, you can construct simple or complex models for slab forms in card before trying to cut and assemble the form in clay.

Lay your template on the firmed-up slab of clay. Using a sharp clay knife, cut around the template. It is best to pull the scrap clay away from the cut shape, leaving the template in place to minimise distortion.

Assembly

The slab form can be assembled once the cut slabs are stiff enough to support themselves without slumping. Cut clay slabs are usually allowed to dry to almost leatherhard stage before being assembled.

Clay slabs must be joined carefully so that the form holds together without cracking or pulling apart during drying and firing. Slabs to be joined need to be at the same stage of dryness; in other words, their moisture content must be equal.

To join slabs:

- Using a pin tool or a toothbrush, score both pieces (roughen the surfaces with crisscross scratches into the clay surface) where the surfaces will contact one another.
- Make a slurry (see below) of the same clay and paint it on the scored marks with a paintbrush.
- Where two pieces join to form an angle place a soft coil of clay along the inside of the join and smooth it into place.
- Blend the outside of the join together with a wooden tool, then smooth it.
- Once all the pieces of the slab form have been assembled and smoothed, wrap the form in plastic and leave it overnight to allow the moisture in all the parts to equalise. Remove the plastic for

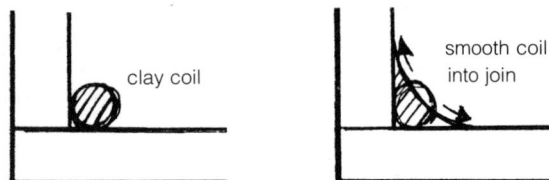

Strengthening slab joins

several hours each day to allow the piece to dry slowly. You can further clean up the joins when the piece has firmed up or is air dry. Scraping with a metal scraper or sanding the piece when it is dry will further refine it.

Slurry is a thick form of liquid clay and is used to join clay surfaces together. Always make slurry (and its thinner version, 'slip'—see page 23) from the same clay as the pot you are working on to ensure compatibility of shrinkage and drying.

To make slurry:
- Break plastic clay into small pieces and dry them. (You may speed the drying by placing the clay in an oven set at 150°C with the door open slightly.
- Once dry, pound the clay between layers of newspaper until it forms a powder.
- Add the clay powder gradually to a container one-third full of water, mixing as you add, until you obtain a smooth consistency like yoghourt. When not in use store slurry in a plastic container with a tightly fitting lid to stop it from drying out.

Coiling

Coils are long, soft sausages of clay that are placed on top of one another, joined together by blending, and paddled with a flat wooden stick to consolidate the form. The advantage of coil-building over pinching is that it enables very large forms to be made. The coil method of making pots continues to be used in both contemporary and primitive cultures worldwide.
- Start by rolling a large number of coils of equal diameter. The size will depend on the size of the pot you wish to make—small, delicate forms require small coils, large forms use fat coils. Clay needs to be of a soft consistency that will not crack easily, and thoroughly wedged.
- Taking a lump of wedged clay, pat into a fat sausage.
- Continue to squeeze the clay between both hands until it forms a sausage about 30 mm thick.
- From this point, you can continue to roll the clay between the palms of your hands to obtain the required thickness. Or you can roll the coils on a slightly dampened absorbent surface (canvas or cement sheeting) using your fingers and palms.

- Starting at the centre of the coil with both hands together, palms down, move lightly outwards along the coil until your hands are at opposite ends of the coil. Start again in the centre, rolling out towards the ends and continue until you get the required thickness.
- Once you have rolled a good quantity of coils, wrap them in a damp cloth or plastic to ensure they remain soft. You are now ready to begin your coil pot.

To form the base:
The base of the coil pot can be a pinch pot, or a rolled slab base, to which coils are added. It is helpful to have a curved bisqued form into which you can lay the slab. (This supports the bottom of the pot and, because it is curved, it will turn easily as you are coiling. When the coiled pot is completed, it can stay in this bisqued form until leatherhard. Since bisqued clay is absorbent, your coil pot will not stick to it.)

To form the pot:
Ensure that the coils of clay are of the same consistency as the base. Avoid using slip or water to join the coils as both will soften and weaken the clay, eventually causing it to collapse. Since the base has to support the weight of the coiled walls (which can be considerable if it is a large pot), the slab needs to be of appropriate thickness.
- Place the first coil around the base, slightly inside the outer edge. Proceed to join by pinching and smearing the base and coil together, on both the inside and outside of the coil. This will create a unified surface.
- Continue to join coils to one another in this manner by laying the next coil on top and pinching and smearing while turning the pot around. If you want the form to curve inwards, place the new coil on the inside of the top rim; if you want the pot to flare out, place the top coil towards the outside of the rim.
- Smooth the surface both inside and out with a rubber kidney or wooden tool with a serrated edge, and consolidate the joins by paddling. If you wish to use a heat gun or a hair dryer to help stiffening the clay as you go, avoid drying the top coil as it will not join properly to the next soft coil unless damp.
- Continue to add coils, pinch and smear, smooth and paddle to build up your form to the required shape. This process requires patience and control—if the form is too soft and you continue to add coils, the combined weight may eventually cause the form to collapse. It is a good idea to have two or three pots on the go simultaneously. While you are working on the other pieces, your first pot has sufficient time to *set up* ready to take the next coil. When a pot is setting up always wrap the rim in plastic to keep it soft enough to

18

take additional coils. Treat the inside of your pot with as much care, smoothing and finishing the joins, as you do the outside. Even if you can't see the inside joins, coils must be properly blended together to prevent cracking from both sides.

- Once the form is complete and has set up, paddle it all over to consolidate the clay and strengthen the surface.
- Slowly dry the pot until leatherhard. You may wish to scrape back the form to even out any bumps and clarify the shape. The tool that works best for this is a flexible metal kidney. Clay is at its most fragile at the dry stage: you would be wise to work on a thin piece of foam to cushion the pot while scraping (and later while sanding).
- Work in any carving or surface texture at this stage.
- When fully dry, refine the piece further by scraping and sanding.

Press- and Drape-moulding

Clay can be draped into or on top of moulds to create a variety of forms. Moulds are useful if you wish to repeat a particular form, make an unusual shape or create rich surface texture.

You can make your own press and drape moulds or use objects that already exist in your kitchen—a gently curving bowl or angled cake tin, or cheap plastic forms of all kinds. If you are going to drape into an existing form, you will need to separate the clay from the mould with a thin layer of plastic to ensure that it will come out of the form easily (the surface will be non-porous and the clay therefore liable to stick). Existing forms can be replicated by being cast in plaster (see *Working with plaster*, page 9) or made out of bisqued clay (pukis).

To make a puki:
- Choose a bowl with an open curve rather than an inward curve, (or you will not be able to get your clay out). Plastic, rounded, shallow bowls are ideal.
- Line or coat it with strips of damp newspaper to ensure the clay does not stick to the bowl.
- Lay slabs of soft clay inside, or drape them on top of, the lined or coated bowls.

Once dried, sanded and bisque-fired, these also make excellent formers in which to start your coil-built bowls (see page 18). They don't stick to the clay and they turn easily, supporting the form you are building.

Formers

Formers are useful for reproducing flat shapes and low bowls any number of times, thus creating sets. For the fish dishes (Project 6), I created formers from styrofoam as it is light, and easily cut, glued and sanded. It is ideal when a flexible shape is needed, as for the wavy lines of the fish dish.

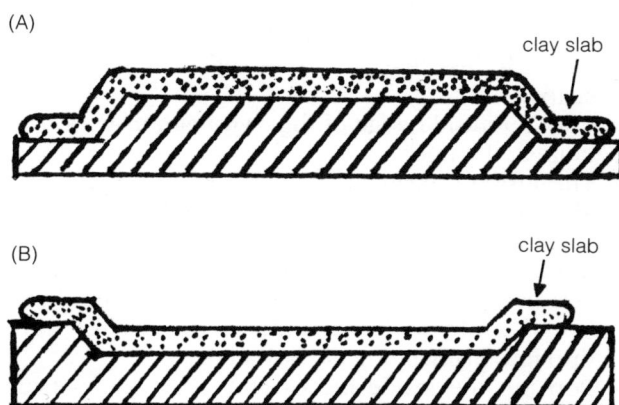

Positive former (A) and negative former (B)

If you want your work to have surface texture or greater variety of form, sand is an interesting medium for creating moulds. The form is made in damp sand, and plaster is carefully poured in to create a positive shape, which is then used as a drape mould once the excess sand is dusted off.

Craftwood, cut and sanded, then sealed with Estapol makes long-lasting, accurate formers. Wooden moulds are useful to create square or rectangular low platters, and moulds made from sheets of styrofoam cut and glued together and sanded smooth will give you great flexibility in making curved or unusual shapes, with the added advantage of being light and easy to store.

To make a negative styrofoam former:
- Draw the shape of your choice (for example, the fish dish in Project 6) onto a piece of card or paper—this will be your template. Lay the template on a piece of 25 mm styrofoam and trace around it with a black felt tip pen.

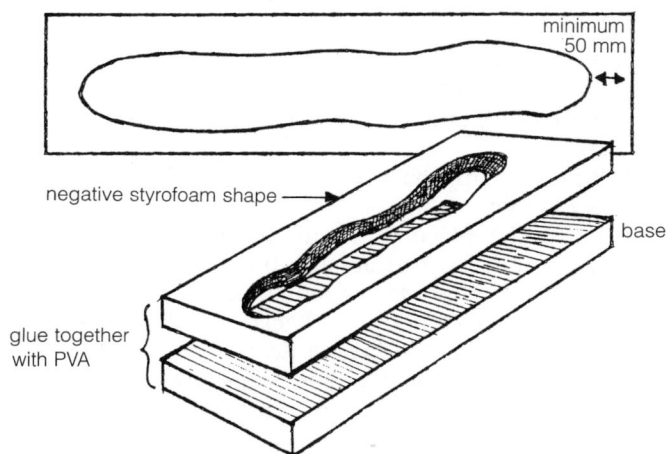

Attach the former to a base board

- Using the metal ruler, draw a frame outside the traced shape on the styrofoam, making sure to allow no less than a 50 mm space all around the shape.
- Cut the outside edge of the styrofoam using a matt knife and a ruler.
- The inside (negative) shape needs to be cut on a 45° angle so that the side is angled. First, lightly score along the line you have made, using a matt knife. Then, angling the knife, cut deeper until you have almost cut through the styrofoam. Use a bread knife to finish cutting or sawing right through, maintaining the 45° angle.
- Pop out the inside pieces and retain the outside piece. Sand the inside angle to smooth.
- To create the base of the dish, cut a flat 25 mm sheet of styrofoam to the same dimensions as the outside edge of the negative shape.
- Glue the base piece to the negative shape with PVA glue. This will create the negative former in which you can drape soft slabs of clay to form your piece.

To make a positive styrofoam former:
- Make a template for the shape you wish to create and transfer onto 25 mm styrofoam.
- Cut around the outside of the shape on a 45° angle with the matt knife.
- Glue this onto a base sheet of 25 mm styrofoam at least 50 mm larger than the shape all the way around.
- Sand to smooth rough edges.

You can make any number of shapes in this way. Being light, styrofoam formers are easy to handle and store. They are inexpensive and will withstand reasonable use.

The clay slabs that you drape over or press into moulds need to be soft in order to take on the shape of the mould without cracking. They also need to have a minimum thickness of 8 mm. Clay slabs that are too thin will warp when fired. Larger pieces require thicker slabs.

To mould clay:
- Press your soft clay slab into, or lay it on top of, the mould, and smooth it into place with a damp sponge.
- When set up, shape further or smooth with a rubber kidney.
- Allow the piece to set up further until you can safely transfer it to another board without altering its shape. Note: forms left in or on a mould too long will crack because the clay shrinks as it dries.
- Trim off excess clay while the piece is in the mould. At the leatherhard stage you can further finish the form and can add feet, handles, lugs, etc. as required.
- Finally, slowly dry the piece to prevent warping and cracking.

Hollowing Out

This method of creating forms produces an organic effect.
- Form a lump of well-wedged clay as a solid piece by rolling, paddling or texturing in a variety of ways.
- Allow the form to firm up on the outside so that it will not distort while being hollowed out. If you wish, you can carve into the outside surface at this stage or wait until the leatherhard stage.
- If the form is a lidded container, cut it to form a top and a bottom. A bowl shape can be made by determining where the rim of the bowl will be and carving inside from the rim down.
- Decide on the thickness you want the walls to be, and mark them by scoring along the top with a pin tool.
- Then, using a small metal looped tool (used for trimming pots thrown on the potter's wheel), scoop out the clay, taking care not to cut too much away at once. Allow the clay to firm up more as the walls get thinner.
- When the piece is almost dry scrape the inside one final time to make it smooth.
- Wipe a sponge around the rim and sand lightly to refine surfaces.
- Burnishing is another way of finishing the outside surface to give a smooth, shiny appearance.

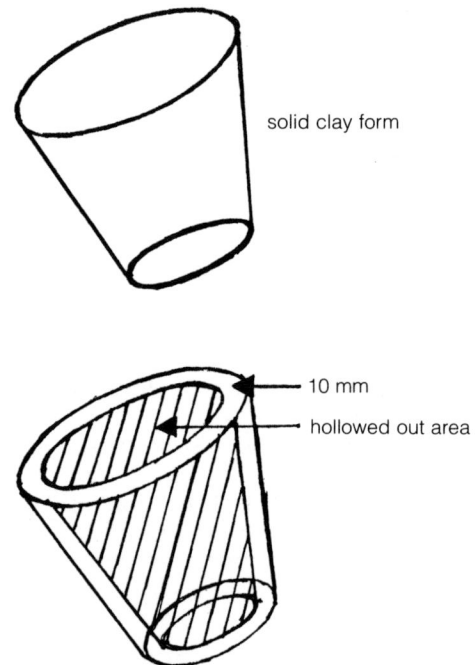

solid clay form

10 mm

hollowed out area

Clay forms can be hollowed out using a small metal looped tool

Decorating Techniques

Surface Texture

Texture is the appearance and feel of the surface of an object—its visual and tactile quality. Clay is an ideal material to express texture as it is malleable and will easily take on a variety of surface effects.

While clay itself has a broad range of textures depending on its type and on the addition of other materials to it, there are also many ways to give surface texture to clay. An understanding of the character of the clay you are using—for instance, is it rough or coarse, smooth or fine?—will give you some direction in creating a texture that will work best.

An ideal way to experiment is to roll out slabs of clay and, using a variety of tools as well as your fingers, try lots of different effects. Then, after allowing your texture swatches to firm up, cut them into tiles and bisque-fire them. These will provide a ready reference for you. It is a good idea to scratch on the back of the tile details of what you used to achieve the texture, so that you may duplicate it. These tiles can also be used to impress texture into soft clay, or to test the effects of glaze.

Texture can be achieved at different stages in the making process, as indicated in the table. Consider the amount and size of the decoration or texture you wish to use in relation to the form of the pot and its scale, so that the surface treatment enhances rather than dominates the finished piece.

Slip trailing

To trail slip onto a firm clay surface, make up the recipe (page 60) and apply with a slip trailer. You can buy this piece of equipment from ceramics suppliers, or make your own from recycled small plastic bottles with very fine-nozzle lids (such as those used for hair-colouring).

Practise slip trailing first on newspaper to get a feel for the technique and to work out the type of lines and patterns you wish to trail. Beware: lumps can form and block the nozzle of the slip trailer. When you squeeze harder, you risk the disappointment of a big blob on your piece! To prevent this, keep the slip trailer sealed tightly when not in use, and always use slip that has been sieved. Also note that too much slip-trailing on a piece can cause it to soften and even collapse.

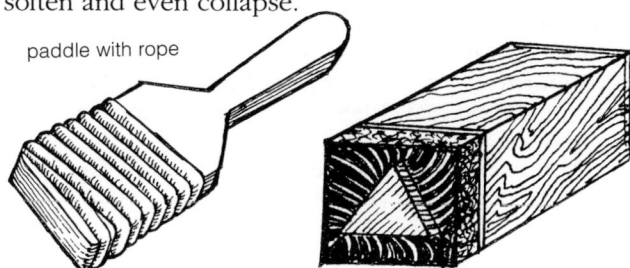

paddle with rope

lino stamp

Texturing clay at different stages

Texturing method \ Clay	Soft	Leather-hard	Dry
Impressing or stamping with carved bisqued stamps or natural objects	✓	✓	
Rolling with bisqued roulettes	✓		
Drawing on with ballpoint pen	✓		
Scoring with various tools, e.g. bamboo skewer	✓		
Stretching	✓		
Cutting with twisted wire or stretched springs	✓		
Poking	✓		
Adding coils	✓		
Cutting or gouging into	✓		
Fluting	✓	✓	
Slip trailing		✓	
Faceting		✓	
Carving		✓	✓
Paddling using textured paddles		✓	
Scratching (sgraffito)		✓	✓
Painting with coloured slips or underglaze		✓	✓
Adding clay		✓	
Scraping		✓	✓
Scratching or carving through slip		✓	
Burnishing		✓	✓
Inlaying slip			✓
Incising lines and dots			✓
Piercing			✓

Burnishing

Burnishing is the polishing of the clay's surface by rubbing, using small circular movements. This seals the surface and makes it shiny, but does not make it watertight. Most clay bodies will burnish, although finer grained clays are most successful. Clay with large particles or grog in the body prove more frustrating to polish, especially when the particles are at surface level. Forms to be burnished should be simple and rounded. At various stages of drying, the clay will respond differently to burnishing—the first polishing is usually done at leatherhard stage, and is followed by additional burnishing up to the dry stage (that is, before bisque-firing).

Different tools may be used for burnishing, from plastic or metal spoons to the palm of your hand! I get most pleasure from using a collection of polished stones of various rounded shapes.

- When leatherhard, burnish your pot with the tool of your choice, then wrap it loosely in plastic.
- Leave it for a few days, until the remaining moisture in the clay causes the surface to swell slightly, thus removing the burnishing dints without spoiling the shine. At this stage, you can burnish some more if you like, the longer you burnish the pot the shinier it will be.
- When the pot is dry give it a final polish using a wad of plastic wrap which has been rolled into a firm ball and covered tightly with more plastic wrap.

Burnished pots should be fired in low-temperature kilns such as sawdust, black fire or pit kilns. First they require bisquing to a temperature of 750°C. The lower firing won't destroy the burnish on the pot; it enhances it, depositing carbon from the smoke produced in the firing into the porous clay body, and giving variations of black and grey to the surface.

Colouring Clay

Clay can be found in a vast array of colours, from the red commonly occurring in earthenware and terracotta clays to the blue-white of some porcelains. Colour in the clay depends on the type of clay, where it is located and the minerals and impurities it contains. The colour of raw clay may change markedly when fired, depending on the temperature it is fired to.

Clays can be mixed and blended to create a broad range of colours. Take care to mix only clays that are compatible in shrinkage and firing temperatures, but also test whenever possible—this is the only clear indication of which clays (and slips) can be mixed together successfully to obtain a variety of colours.

As well as blending clays of existing colours, you can add oxides or stains to light-coloured clays to achieve a rich palette of colours. Take care when preparing coloured clays. Place plastic down before starting. Clean all surfaces when finished. Do not eat or drink while working. Wear a mask when weighing dry ingredients.

Oxides

!
CAUTION

Raw materials in the form of metallic oxides are used in clay and glaze for a number of purposes. Twelve metallic oxides are commonly used as colourants. Oxides added to clay are more subdued and limited in colour than the processed stains, but are generally a less expensive form of colourant. Some oxides are toxic and require care in use.

Stains

Ceramic stains (prepared mixtures of colouring oxides, stabilisers and modifiers) are used for colouring not only clay bodies but also slips, underglaze (see page 23) and glaze. The coarser particle size is used for colouring clay bodies and slips and the finer particle size used for colouring glaze and underglaze.

Stains are available from ceramic suppliers as fine powders, with a wide range of colours offered. They fire to high temperatures without losing their colour; in fact, they usually darken slightly. They are more stable than raw oxides and may be mixed with one another to produce greater subtlety and variation in colour. Being more highly refined than oxides, they mix more easily into the clay, slip or glaze, with less tendency to speckle.

Mixing stains

Most stains are compatible with each other. Suppliers will tell you which colours do not mix.

Stains are expensive, so you need to maximise the colours you have. By obtaining a few basic colours plus black, you can create a good range of shades and tints. To darken a colour, add very small amounts of black stain (shade). To lighten a colour, increase the amount of white slip in the mix (tint). To intensify the colour, add more stain to the mix. You can create a colour tonal range by doing a lineblend of two colours, for example (where R=red and G=green):

100% Red	10G 90R	20G 80R	30G 70R	40G 60R	50G 50R	60G 40R	70G 30R	80G 20R	90G 10R	100% Green

To add colour to clay:

- Using a white earthenware, stoneware or porcelain clay to obtain the brightest colour response, make up the required number of 500 g balls.
- Cover in plastic until ready to use.
- Prepare the oxides/stains ready for use by weighing out small amounts of each to add to the clay. I prefer the teaspoon method, judging by eye to obtain the desired colour.
- Record the amount you have put in each ball and make a coded sample tile for future reference and duplication.
- Press a hole into the centre of your ball of clay with your thumb, add the required amount of stain or oxide and a teaspoon of water (or more as needed to wet the powder).
- Repeat this method with all the balls.
- Mix the stain into a paste inside the ball of clay with a brush.
- Carefully close over the hole by pinching the ball of clay together again on top, trapping the mixed stain inside.
- Using both hands, squeeze and knead the ball to blend the colour in thoroughly. This is a messy procedure, so you will need to work on a sheet of plastic. The colour must be evenly dispersed throughout the ball, with no speckles or lumps remaining. If the colour does not look dark enough you may wish to add more—keep track of the total amount added.
- Wrap each coloured ball separately in plastic wrap

and store in a sealed plastic container until you are ready to use them, as clay containing oxides and stains tends to dry out quickly.

Coloured slip

While it is valuable to be able to create pots whose coloured patterns come from the clay body itself, colour can also be painted onto pots. This is done by using liquid clay, known as 'slip' as a white base to which colour is added in the form of oxides and stains. (Slip is a thin version of slurry. To make slip, follow the instructions for making slurry on page 18, but thin with water until it has the consistency of cream.)

Using coloured slips allows for greater variation in colour and decorating techniques, enabling the student to explore in these areas before having an in-depth understanding of glaze.

Slip may be made from any light-coloured clay. The clay you use will alter the colour of the stain—the whiter the clay, the brighter the colour. Coloured slip may be poured, painted, trailed, marbellised, scratched through, scraped back, inlayed, or applied 'in resist' (over waxed areas that resist underglaze or slip; this produces a stencilled effect), to name a few of its many decorative uses. Clear glaze may then be applied over the top to seal the ware (see *Glazing*, page 26), providing an easily cleaned surface that makes the piece practical to use. Clear glaze usually intensifies the colour of the slip.

To add colour to slip:
- Slip may be made in large batches, e.g. 2 litres, ahead of time, then divided into smaller amounts for the colour to be added.
- Store the slip in plastic containers with tightly fitting lids to prevent it from thickening or drying up. Label clearly.
- Weigh out the stain or oxide and record the amount of dry material you are adding to the amount of liquid slip, e.g. 2 tsp stain to 250 ml slip.
- Pour the dry stain into the wet slip and mix thoroughly with a bristle brush. Sieve twice through a 120-mesh sieve to distribute the colour evenly and prevent speckling.
- Slip for colouring and painting must be the consistency of thickened cream. It should coat your fingernail when you dip your finger into it.
- Slip for slip-trailing needs to be slightly thicker than for painting or pouring.

It is useful to punch a hole in your samples. Once fired, these samples can be hung on a board or attached to your buckets of coloured slip for easy reference. Eventually you will settle on a firing temperature that best suits your needs. Then further colour blends may be done to achieve a complete palette of possible colours.

To carve through slip:
- Using either dark or white slip, paint leatherhard pots where you want the carved decoration to be. Allow to set up. Using a pin tool or a bamboo skewer, lightly outline the design you wish to carve out. It is helpful to sketch a few ideas on paper before drawing your design into the clay.
- Using a clay carving tool, follow the lines you have drawn, carve through the slip to the clay body underneath, leaving the areas you wish to remain dark or light (depending on the slip you have chosen). Work slowly, being careful not to carve too deeply into the wall or you will weaken the pot.
- Allow to dry, then gently dust off any dry burrs (rough bits of clay stuck to the surface). The pot is now ready for firing.

Testing colours

Testing and recording is the best way to determine the amounts you will need to use to obtain certain colours, and the effect firing will have on these colours.

To test oxides and stains try firing them at a variety of temperatures; cones 012, 07, 2, 6, 8, will give you a sampling of colours obtainable at those temperatures. An electric kiln is more suitable for testing, providing a *neutral* (cleaner) atmosphere, although tests can be done in a gas kiln to determine the differences in colour that can be achieved.

Always make a sample disc from each ball of coloured clay you produce to fire at different temperatures, or have small bisqued tiles to paint coloured slip on for firing. If you glaze half the tile with clear glaze you will be able to see both glazed and unglazed colour response on one tile.

Underglaze

Underglaze is a mixture of ceramic stain and *frit*, finely ground. It may be painted onto raw or bisqued clay which is then clear-glazed. Underglaze is useful as colour for painted decoration at a variety of firing temperatures. It may be airbrushed onto bisqued clay and I find it useful added to porcelain clay or slips to create a wide palette of colours.

Underglaze powder must be mixed with a medium (available at ceramics suppliers—see page 61) in order to be painted onto raw or bisqued clay. Colours can be mixed as for stains (see page 22), but to tint an underglaze colour (that is, make it pastel), add a white underglaze powder rather than a slip.

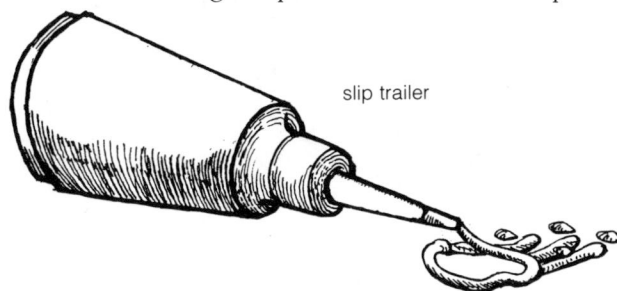
slip trailer

Marbellising

You can marbellise two or more coloured clays together by wedging them. The longer you wedge, the more the colours will mix, so it is best to experiment first to obtain the results you prefer. Colours that contrast with one another (for example, black/white, brown/red, blue/white) will give clearer results. To see how the two colours are mixing, wire cut your ball of clay after you have wedged it two or three times. When you are satisfied with the effect, roll or pinch the clay into a pot. Once dry, scrape the clay with a metal kidney to clarify the marbellised pattern. Do not sand the clay or you will smear the marbellising.

Laminating and Neriage

Contrasting clays may be layered in a number of ways using related processes known as laminating and neriage.

Laminating involves rolling thin layers of varying colours of clay, cutting them into shapes or patterns, and laying them on a base slab of clay. They are then rolled into the base slab.

Neriage is a Japanese decorative technique. Thin slabs of contrasting clays are layered one on top of another, creating blocks of patterns. The blocks are cut end-on and pressed into simple moulds to form repeat patterns which can be very intricate. Stained porcelain clays can produce colourful neriage patterns.

Laminating method

- Using the uncoloured clay body with which you are building your pot, roll a base slab of clay to 10 mm thick.
- Roll fine slabs about 2 mm thick using a variety of colours which have been added to the base clay. Cut into shapes, roll into narrow coils or form into small balls to create shapes, lines and dots. Place

Patterning the inside of a clay ball

these on the base slab, lay newspaper on top, and carefully roll into the base (the coils will flatten into lines, the balls into dots). To equalise the moisture levels of the differently coloured clays, store the laminated slab in plastic until you are ready to construct your piece. Dry very slowly before firing.

Neriage method

- Roll slabs of differently coloured clay to 2 mm thick.
- Paint each slab with slip, then lay a contrasting slab on top. The slip helps the layers of clay to stick together.
- Gently roll with a rolling pin after each layer to ensure no air is trapped between the layers (trapped air will cause the neriage to split open when drying).
- Store the neriage block in plastic until you are ready to construct your piece.

Patterning the surface of a clay ball:
- Cut slices 2 mm thick from the neriage block described above, or form coloured shapes, coils or small balls as described above, and apply these to the surface of a ball of clay. Roll the ball smooth again before pinching to form a pot.

Patterning the inside of a clay ball:
- Cut a ball of clay in half. Between the two halves place a slice of contrasting clay or a slice from a neriage block of about the same size as the ball. Press the halves back together and pat round again.

If you make an opening hole at the top of the unpatterned section, down through the centre to about 10 mm from the bottom, the pattern will appear around the circumference of the pot, both inside and outside, as the pot is pinched out. Scraping with a metal kidney will clarify the pattern. (Do not sand, or the pattern will smear.)

Neriage block

24

Drying and Firing Clay

Drying Clay

The drying of clay is an ongoing process which begins with air drying and is completed during the early stages of firing.

Water can account for up to forty per cent of the weight of plastic clay. For this reason, clay feels cold and damp to the touch when not completely dry. Clay is at its leatherhard stage when it is stiff but still contains some moisture. As more water evaporates during air drying, all the clay particles come into contact with one another, and the pot shrinks, lightens in colour and feels dry, not cool to touch. At this stage *drying shrinkage* is complete and the clay is called *greenware*.

To avoid warping or cracking during drying, it is important to dry objects made of clay *slowly* and evenly. Proper drying of your work is essential to prevent warping, pulling apart of joins or cracking.

The size of your piece and variations in thickness or mass will determine the length of time required for the piece to be thoroughly and evenly dried. Drying means *shrinkage*; if one part of your work is drying faster than the other, the tension created by different rates of shrinkage will cause the piece to warp and crack. Hence the importance of careful drying over a period of time, and allowing air to get to all parts of the piece, even underneath. Placing work on small slats of wood, or turning the piece upside-down to allow the bottom to be exposed to air helps air circulation and even drying. To allow for even drying, wrap work loosely in plastic, or place it in a drying cupboard (see page 11), and expose it to air for short periods of time each day, increasing the exposure time over a week until the plastic can be removed completely.

Air temperature, humidity and circulation all affect the rate of drying. Clay temperature also plays a part. A draught or a fan blowing directly onto one side of a piece is bound to create stress, but using a hot-air blower or a heat gun to stiffen a piece as you work on it will not cause problems providing the piece is constantly turned to allow all sides to set up evenly. The best policy you can adopt is to allow plenty of time for drying!

The stage of drying that follows air drying occurs during the first firing in the kiln, as the temperature is slowly rising to 400°C. Called *steaming* or *water smoking*, this is the stage at which all the uncombined water in the clay will have evaporated and the clay will be fully dry (called *bone dry*). If this process does not occur slowly, with the lid of the kiln slightly open and air ports open, formation of steam within

the clay may cause it to burst. Thick cross-sections increase the danger of an explosion.

Often, a smell is associated with this stage of firing, as most clays contain vegetable matter, which decomposes up to 580°C.

Between 350° and 700°C, the bound or chemically combined water, which is part of the crystal structure of the clay, is driven off. Meanwhile, by about 600°C, the clay has become completely dehydrated and will no longer slake down or dissolve in water. It has lost its plasticity and is very fragile, with slight shrinkage. This stage is known as the *ceramic change*.

At 573°C, quartz (also known as silica) crystals undergo a change from alpha to beta quartz, marked by a sudden increase in volume. Upon cooling, the crystals revert to their original form. Through both heating and cooling stages, take care to proceed slowly, so as to prevent cracking or *dunting*.

By 1000°C, oxidation (see page 15) or decomposition of all components of clay not already in oxide form, occurs (for example, organic and inorganic carbonates and sulphates). If proper oxidation does not happen—that is, if there is not enough air in the kiln—a blackening or discolouration will be noticed: carbon remains in the fired pieces. This undesirable result, which tends to occur in kilns fuelled by gas, oil or wood rather than electricity, weakens the fired body and may cause bloating when higher temperatures are reached. You can detect 'black core', as it is known, by breaking open a piece and examining the cross-section to see whether it is black in the middle. Slowing the pace of the firing between 750°C and 1000°C will prevent carbon from being trapped in the clay.

Fusion of the clay, having begun at 800°C, proceeds until the maturing temperature of the clay is reached. Vitrification, as this is called at its final point, imparts to the clay the hard, durable, dense and rock-like properties of ceramics. Vitrification is accompanied by shrinkage in the clay. The melting of the oxides (fusion) takes place gradually, depending on the temperature to which the clay is fired. The maturing temperature is reached slowly over a period of time according to the general instructions for firing a kiln and the type of clay and glaze you are using.

Note: The *firing shrinkage* of clay is equal to the *drying shrinkage*.

Generally clay is fired twice—the first firing is known as bisque firing and the second as glaze firing. Unglazed pots such as the mini herb pots on page 46 require a single, high-temperature firing only.

Bisque-firing

The first firing, done when the pots are air dry, hardens the clay but allows it to remain porous and capable of accepting glaze. Bisque temperatures vary depending on your final method of firing. Generally,

25

for pots that are to be glazed with earthenware or stoneware glazes, the bisque temperatures range from 950°C to 1020°C. The recommended bisque and glaze temperatures are specified on most packs of clay.

For primitive-style kilns such as pit, blackfire, sawdust and raku kilns, the bisque temperature needs to be lower—700°C to 850°C—to allow the carbon to saturate the clay (this does not apply to high-temperature firings) and to prevent cracking.

In the bisque firing pots can be stacked touching, inside each other or stacked one on top of the other because there is no glaze on the pots to stick them together.

Both bisque and glaze firings commence slowly with a preheat of the kiln. This is undertaken with the peepholes open and the door or lid of the kiln may be slightly ajar to allow steam to escape.

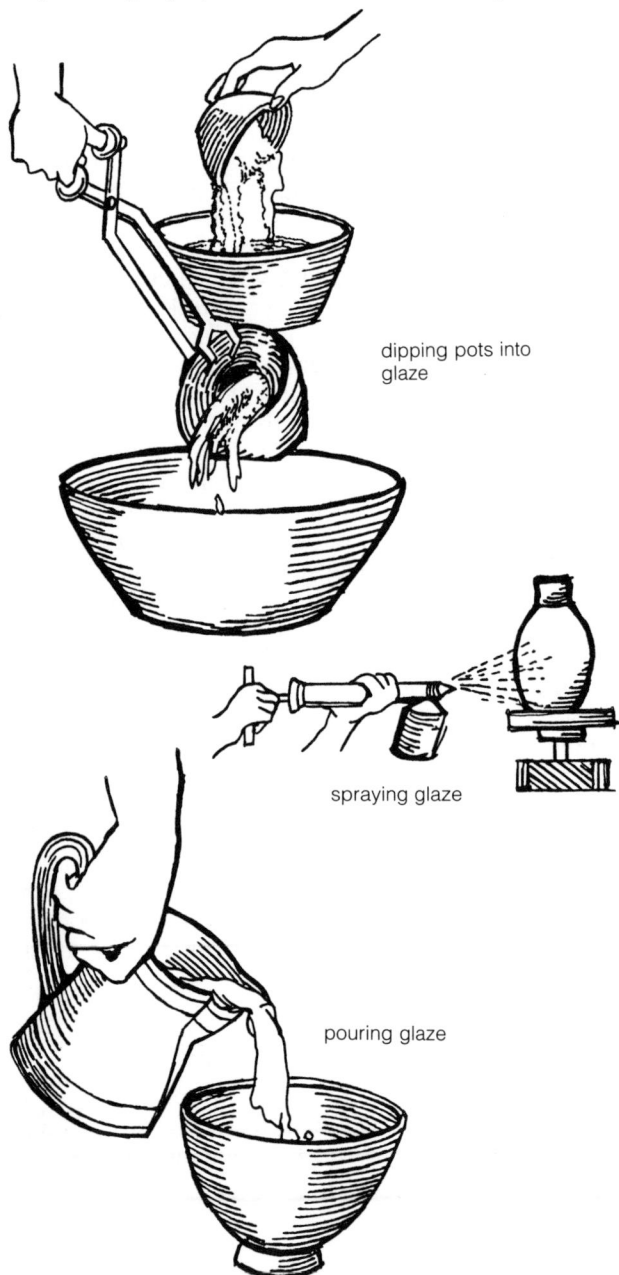

dipping pots into glaze

spraying glaze

pouring glaze

Glazing

It is standard practice to glaze work only after it has been bisqued (see page 25). While pots can be glazed at leatherhard or dry stages, glazes and procedures need to be modified to suit the single-firing (such modifications are beyond the scope of this book). Bisqued work is much easier to handle.

Read the section *Working with Glaze*, page 7, before embarking on any work that requires glazing.

Before you glaze:
- Ensure that all bisqued work is clean and dust-free by dipping it in clean warm water and allowing it to dry. Dust on the surface will cause glaze to pinhole or crawl.
- Limit handling of the work—greasy fingers will leave areas that resist glaze.
- Always wax the bottom of your work, or any area that will be in contact with the kiln shelf (for example, feet). You do this by brushing on a liquid wax emulsion or hot paraffin wax.

The instructions for all projects in this book assume that you have taken the above steps before glazing your work.

Methods of Application

Glaze is commonly applied to work by dipping, pouring or spraying—or by combining any of these methods. Dipping and pouring are the most economical. Painting is another way of applying glaze, but it is slower and may result in uneven glaze application.

Always mix up enough glaze to cover all your work. Ensure that the glaze is of the right consistency (see page 8) before pouring or dipping, and that the bottom of your work is waxed.

Size and type of work will help to determine the method of glaze application. How easily can the work be held for dipping? Perhaps the work is too large for pouring or dipping and will require spraying. Intricate detail may be obscured by pouring, and very thin delicate work calls for careful application of glaze, probably by spraying. Work that has been bisque-fired too high will be more difficult to glaze, as the fired clay will be less porous. If this occurs, heat your work to 150°C in an oven to make the surface more receptive, and glaze while warm.

To dip or pour:
- First pour glaze inside the work, swill around and quickly pour out. Wipe off excess drips, then leave the pots overnight to allow the inside glaze to dry thoroughly.
- Glaze the outside of the work by holding the piece level to prevent glaze going inside, and dip top-down into the glaze. If the pot is small enough or you have mixed enough glaze, you can glaze the outside in one dip. Otherwise, wait for the top

of the piece to be dry enough to hold, turn the pot over and dip the bottom half.
- Wipe any excess glaze from the bottom of your work.

Note: Work quickly to prevent too thick a layer of glaze from forming. Pouring or dipping different glazes over one another can produce interesting and sometimes beautiful effects. Testing will provide useful information.

To spray:

!
CAUTION

- Check that the glaze is smoothly mixed and thoroughly sieved—lumps will clog your equipment.
- Thin the glaze with water to ease application.
- Fill your spray gun and use according to the instructions. Remember that inhalation of airborne glaze particles is a health hazard. Work in a proper spray booth with an extractor fan (see page 12).

Spraying glaze allows you to apply thin, even coats of glaze with greater control over the results.

The high cost of spray equipment, the need for special spraying facilities, and the risk to health and safety make this method of glaze application unsuitable for beginners. However, the special effects that can be achieved by spraying—soft gradation of colours, even texture, overlaying of varying colours and masking off areas before spraying—make the necessary equipment well worth the investment for more experienced ceramicists.

Decorative Glazing

Decorative effects using glaze may be achieved in a number of ways. Pouring or dipping different glazes on top of one another, trailing glaze in a slip trailer, sponge stamping, and using wax or paper resist are methods worth exploring. Books are available to guide you in these processes (see *Further Reading*, page 63).

Clean-up

!
CAUTION

After a glazing session, it is important to clean your brushes, sieves and buckets thoroughly before glaze dries on them. Wipe down benches and work areas, wash away any dry material spills and store glaze buckets with lids tightly in place. Collect and dispose of any toxic materials (for example, copper or manganese) as described on page 11.

cone pack

Glaze-firing

This second firing takes the clay and glaze to their maturing temperature. This temperature is higher than the bisque temperature.

Preparing for Firing

As glaze will melt and fuse pots to kiln shelves, certain care must be taken in loading a glaze firing. Clean any debris from your kiln shelves and paint them with *kiln wash*—a mixture of calcined alumina and kaolin (see page 60). This gives the shelves a protective coating, making glaze spills easier to remove.

Before loading your work into the kiln check all pieces for drips or splashes of glaze that might have formed on the bottom. An extra precaution against sticking is to mix some clay with a bit of alumina (called a wadding mix—see page 60), roll it into small balls and attach these to the bottom of each piece to elevate it slightly from the shelf during firing.

Stacking and Loading the Kiln

Place three props in a triangle on the floor of the kiln. Place a shelf on top, and position three more props directly above those on the kiln floor. Place pots for firing on the shelf, then put a second shelf on top resting on the props. Continue until stacking is complete.

Load your pieces so that they are not touching.

Controlling Temperature

You use pyrometers and cones to judge the temperature inside your kiln.

Cones are small elongated pyramids of ceramic materials with a known melting point. (They bend when they have reached their given temperature.) You place these in front of the peep holes on the top and bottom shelves to judge the temperature reached, and at various positions inside the kiln (top and bottom, back and front) to judge the evenness of the firing. Cones are made up (and used) in packs of three or four with varying temperatures—the required temperature cone is in the centre and higher and lower temperature cones are on either side. The lower temperature cones serve as a warning that the kiln is approaching the desired temperature, and the higher temperature cones act as insurance against over-firing. The symbol '∆' is a shorthand reference for cone.

Pyrometers are electronic devices that measure the temperature inside the kiln. They are wired into the switching device inside electric kilns, or can be obtained separately for use in gas and other types of kilns. You should always use cones in your kiln as backup.

- Preheat the kiln to about 400°C, then plug the peepholes. It is important that firing proceeds slowly, with rises in temperature no greater than 200°C per hour.
- Once the kiln has reached the required temperature, soak the kiln—that is, maintain the kiln at its top temperature—for half an hour to an hour. Soaking ensures a smooth glaze finish.
- Shut it down and allow it to cool slowly.

After Firing

Unloading

While you may be anxious to see the results of your firing, it is important to allow the kiln to cool fully before unpacking it. Burnt fingers and split pots do not deter some of us from unloading the kiln while it is still too hot to handle but patience will be rewarded!

- To speed up cooling you may open the peepholes, and open the kiln door or lid a crack. But do not do this before the kiln has cooled to 250°C.
- Continue to open the door or lid wider until the kiln is fully cool. When you can touch the pots without burning your fingers, you may remove them from the kiln.

Keeping Records

It is useful to draw or write down where pieces were located in the kiln before unloading them. This information could be valuable for future use.

It is also a good idea to record your firings in your kiln, particularly if the kiln is new and you are unaccustomed to its workings. This can be done either by graph or in note form and should show the time/temperature rate of climb. Whichever method you use, maintaining a *standard* format of recording will enable you to compare results and reproduce the successful effects of a particular firing cycle. Kiln logs are also a useful way of determining whether elements need replacement through wear, or of trouble shooting any problems that may occur (with a gas kiln, in particular).

Projects for the Kitchen

Ⓒ
Ⓑ
Ⓐ
1   Spoon Rests

A spoon rest, made from rolled slabs of clay, has many flat surfaces on which to explore simple decorating techniques using coloured slips or slips of contrasting clays. When a clear glaze is applied and fired, the result is a useful and decorative item for the kitchen.

Materials

Terracotta earthenware (I used Delclay)
White earthenware clay (I used Clayworks SWE earthenware/stoneware blend)
A cardboard template
A tablespoon or wooden spoon for impressing into centre of slab
Slip trailer
Flat boards (slightly absorbent) to dry spoon rests on
White and coloured slip to decorate clay (see page 60)
Underglazes (see page 23)
Paraffin wax or liquid wax emulsion.

To form

- Pat clay flat to about 20 mm thick and roll a number of slabs to a thickness of 10–12 mm (see *Clay slabs*, page 17).
- Place slabs on plasterboard or cement sheeting to stiffen while making templates.
- Draw the shape of spoon rest to the size illustrated on cardboard and cut out—this is your template.
- Lay the template on the clay slab and lightly outline (see *Templates*, page 17) repeating to create a number of spoon rests.
- Using a spoon, press into the centre of each shape to create the depression where the spoon will rest. (Do this before you cut out the shape; if you do it afterwards the outside edge will distort.)
- Allow the clay to stiffen for a few hours, then cut the shape out with a clay knife, following your outlines.
- Make a hole at the top of the spoon rest, 10 mm from the edge, using a wooden skewer or nail. (If you place the hole too close to the edge, it will split when drying.) Clean the burred edges of the hole while the clay is leatherhard.

To dry

- Place two sheets of newspaper on a flat board.
- Lay the spoon rests on the newspaper and place two more sheets of newspaper on top.
- Place on top of the newspaper a board the same size as the bottom board.
- Continue to 'sandwich' in this manner (a number of boards may be placed on top of one another)—the weight helps the clay slabs to stay flat. If slabs are of even thickness, and not too thin, there is less chance of warping.
- Turn occasionally to facilitate even drying. Dry slowly.

To clean up

- When air dry, lightly sponge the spoon rests around the edges to smooth. Clean the holes by sanding and sponging. Any surface marks can be lightly sanded.

To decorate

- While the spoon rests are drying you may wish to make up a variety of coloured slips (see *Colouring Clay*, page 23), or you may choose to use white slip on terracotta clay. The terracotta clay may also be made into a slip by drying the clay, crushing between layers of newspaper, and adding the clay to water. Mix to the consistency of thickened cream. Sieve to remove lumps, then paint, pour or trail onto your work.
- While the clay is soft or leatherhard you can draw into it with a bamboo skewer, a ballpoint pen or a pin tool.
- At leatherhard or dry stage, you can apply coloured slip by pouring it onto the slabs; by painting it into an incised pattern; or by painting on and scratching a pattern into it while it is still

A decorated spoon rest

slightly damp. Alternatively, you can cut sponges into simple geometric shapes, dip them into the slip, then stamp them onto the clay surface. Finally, slip may be trailed on using a slip trailer to create lines. Use of strong, contrasting colours will give maximum effect. Words or messages can be painted on or scratched through slip.
• Set aside decorated spoon rests to dry thoroughly.
• Clean brushes thoroughly, and seal slip containers tightly.

To bisque
• Stack spoon rests side-on in the kiln (they may lean against each other).
• Bisque-fire in an electric kiln to 1000°C.

To glaze
• Use earthenware clear gloss (see page 60) or commercial clear glaze CEG-01.
• Wash, and wax bottoms as described on page 26.
• Pour glaze onto spoon rests by holding spoon rest on an angle and pouring glaze from the top down; or dip spoon rest into a bowl of glaze, then drain on an angle.
• Allow to dry.
• When dry, clean excess glaze from the sides and bottom of the spoon rest.

To load and fire
• Load, and fire in an electric kiln to 1060°C.

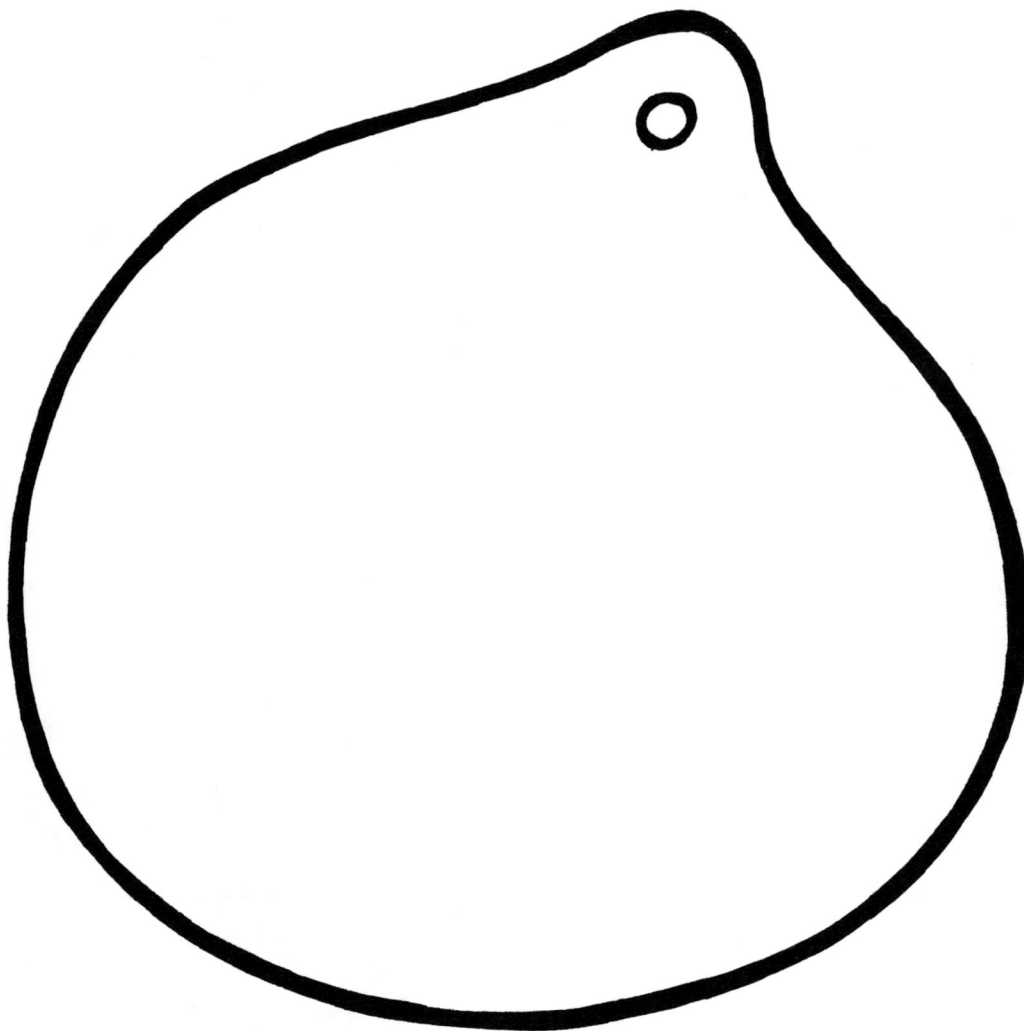

Spoon rest template

Ⓒ
Ⓑ # 2 *Hot Plate Stands*
Ⓐ

Having mastered rolling slabs and accurate cutting, you are ready to move on to joining coils to slabs, or slabs to one another. This project, which results in a set of decorative stands for hot serving plates, will allow you to explore flattened coils and a variety of approaches to making and adding a foot or base to a slab of clay. A number of decorative surfaces will challenge the more experienced reader.

Materials

White earthenware clay
Terracotta earthenware

To form hot plate stands using slabs

- Roll slabs to 10 mm thick (see *Clay slabs*, page 17).
- Allow slabs to stiffen slightly. Meanwhile, try out on newspaper some simple shapes the size you wish to make the hot plate stands, and transfer your successful drawings to light card—these are your templates (see *Templates*, page 17).
- Place the templates on the clay slabs and lightly trace a line around them with a pin tool.
- Using a bamboo skewer, draw lines, patterns, messages, drawings of animals or fruit into the surface of the clay slab while it is fairly soft, for painting in later with coloured slips.
- Allow slabs to stiffen for an hour, then cut along the edges with a clay knife.
- Remove the slabs to cement sheeting to set up until leatherhard. Turn upside-down, ready to attach feet, then cover loosely with plastic to prevent warping.

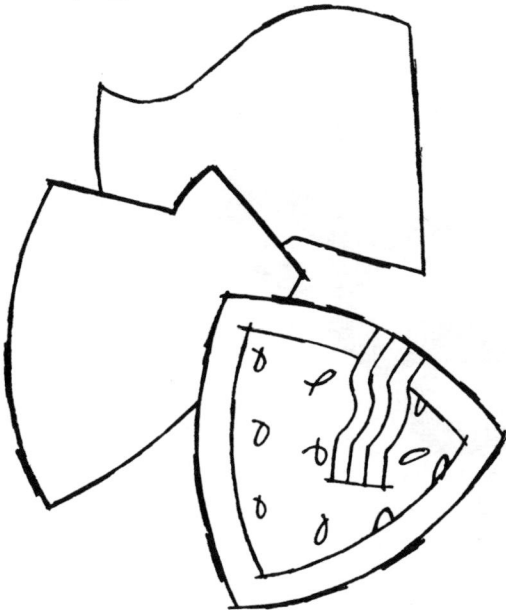

Many shapes are suitable to form hot plate stands

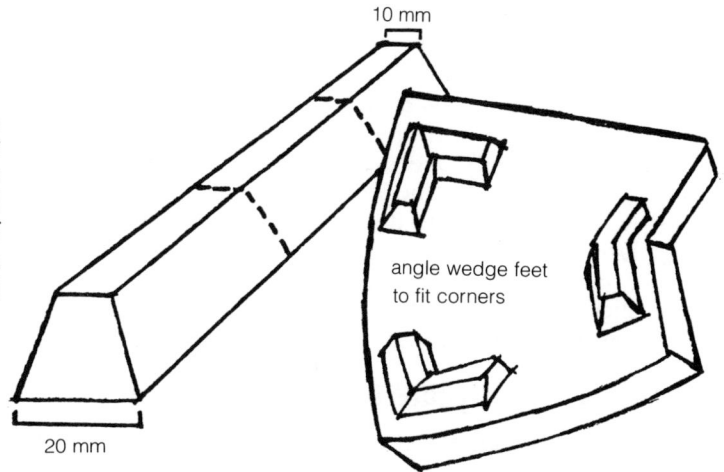

Wedge-shaped feet cut from a slab

To form slab feet

Note: Three feet are often more stable and easier to balance than four.

- Roll out clay to a slab 20 mm thick.
- While soft, cut the clay into wedges 10 mm wide on top and 20 mm wide on the bottom.
- The strip wedges will vary in length—you may cut them and bend them to fit the shape of the hot plate stand or angle them around the corners.

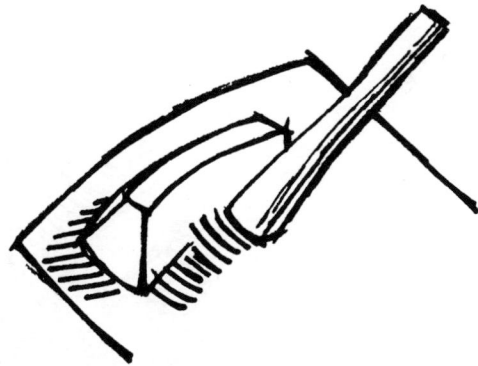

Joining wedge foot

- Lay the wedge-shaped feet in place on the undecorated side of the slab and lightly draw around them with a pin tool.
- Remove the feet from the slab one at a time. Using the pin tool, score lines in the area where the foot will be to roughen the surface of the slab. Paint onto the roughened area a thickened slip or slurry made from the clay you are using (see page 18).
- Place the foot on the roughened area and press. Using a flat wooden tool, join the soft foot to the slab by dragging clay from the foot down onto the slab. Do this around the entire foot, smooth the join and sponge clean. Repeat for all feet.

- Carefully turn the hot plate stand over and place a small wooden board or cement sheeting on top. Press gently to even up the feet. If you press too hard you will warp the slab.
- Turn the slab over again (feet side up), wrap loosely in plastic and leave overnight.
- Remove plastic and dry work slowly, turning regularly. To prevent warping, stand your work on cement sheeting, place another piece of cement sheeting on top with a weight on it, and leave for a week. Check and turn when required.

To form hot plate stands using woven, flattened coils

- Roll a number of coils (at least twelve) of approximately the same diameter, about 250 mm in length (see *Coiling*, page 18). You may texture the coils by rolling them on a textured surface, using a ridged wooden butter paddle to obtain lines in the coils, or rolling the edge of a ruler along the coil to give it a spiral indentation.
- Wrap the coils in plastic until ready for use so that they don't dry out.
- Place a sheet of newspaper on a piece of cement sheeting or plasterboard and lay half of the coils side by side, 10–15 mm apart.
- Working at right angles to the coils on the board, weave another coil over and under them. Don't worry about uneven edges—you can trim them later.

- Weave in the remaining coils one at a time but opposite to the previous coil to achieve a basket-weave effect.
- Gently lay a sheet of newspaper on top of the woven coils, then using a rolling pin, flatten the coils by rolling on top of the newspaper. Press and roll lightly, being careful not to flatten the coils too much—about 10–12 mm thick is ideal.
- Pull the newspaper off the surface, check that all coils are evenly flattened, then trim the edges using a clay knife.
- Remove the woven coils to sheets of dry plasterboard, or place them on sheets of newspaper with a board on top, and allow to set up overnight.
- Form feet using either of the two methods below.

To form loop style feet

- Roll a number of coils textured as described on page 32.
- Cut the number of feet you require to the same length then bend into loops, joining the ends together. Allow to set up slightly.

To join feet to base:

- With a pin tool, score the area where the feet are to be attached. Paint with clay slurry, then press onto the base of the hot plate stand from inside the loop where the coil ends have been joined. You may wish to place the coils on an angle at the corners of the plate stand.

Hot plate stand—woven, flattened coil method

Three individual herb pots are shaped like small birds with the herbs growing from the back of each bird. Beneath the pots are small saucers to catch excess water.

The bonsai planter features geometric lines executed in heavily textured stoneware clay. The simple shape of the planter emphasises the tortured beauty of the bonsai tree.

Whether planted with chillies and herbs (as pictured)
or even a showy cactus, the surface texture and colour
of this pedestal planter may be varied to show to best
advantage any plant. This piece would be a stunning
focal point for a summer luncheon in the garden.

A section of the hanging garden screen is shown here
with the large herb garden planter. This softly coloured
planter is ideal for growing herbs in a patio setting.
Individual pieces of the screen, made from terracotta
clay, are show strewn on the brick paving.

The large fruit bowl painted in blue, yellow and pink slips, and a smaller slip-decorated bowl are clear-glazed for functional use. The six candlesticks, single, double and triple, are made with terracotta or white earthenware clays. Some of the candlesticks have small birds perched on top, bold patterns or leaves and vines winding around the base. The candlesticks may be glazed or unglazed depending on the desired effect. Indoor and outdoor dining will be enhanced by the special atmosphere created by candleholders such as these!

- When all coil loops are joined to the base, turn the hot plate stand over and gently press to ensure that it sits level on its feet. Be careful not to flatten the coil loops or they will break.

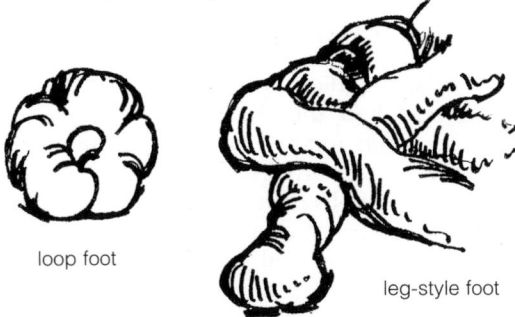

loop foot

leg-style foot

To form leg-style feet

- Roll and texture the coils as for loop-style feet.
- Cut the number of feet you require to the same length—about 35 mm long.
- Taking each length of coil in turn, flatten and widen one end by holding the coil and pressing the other end in a circular motion on a flat surface until it thickens and splays out. This will create the 'foot' end of the leg.
- When all the feet are made, attach them either by placing the fat end on the base of the hot plate stand, giving the effect of a 'pointy' foot, or placing the thin end on the base, allowing the fatter bit to make a foot, much like an elephant's foot.
- When all feet are attached, using the scoring/slurry method of joining (see above), turn your work over and gently press down so that it will sit level on its feet.
- Cover loosely with plastic and allow to dry very slowly.
- Once dry, sponge lightly to smooth surfaces.

To bisque

- Bisque-fire in an electric kiln to 1000°C.

To decorate

The slab hot plate stands formed from terracotta or white earthenware clay will be ready for decoration from leatherhard to dry stage.

- Fill your drawn designs with a dark coloured slip (black is often used to provide an outline), or a mixture of copper oxide or copper carbonate and water, painted along the lines until they are filled—you may need to paint, allow to dry, then fill again with the mixture.
- Allow the slabs to dry. Using a damp sponge, wash back the slip or copper by moving across the lines so that the mixture is removed only from the surface.
- Decorate terracotta pieces using your choice of coloured slips. (You may leave them unglazed.)
- Decorate white earthenware pieces by painting with your choice of coloured slips or with underglaze mixed with medium.
- Bisque-fire, then apply a clear earthenware glaze (see page 60).
- The woven, flattened-coil plate stands must be bisque-fired before being glazed.

Note: Copper carbonate is toxic. Do not ingest. When dry-mixing into a glaze batch do not inhale. When painting onto pieces, take care in handling, avoid contact with mouth. Sponge up any spills immediately.

!
CAUTION

To glaze woven hot plate stands

- Mix up a zircon white glaze (see page 60). You will need to make about 1000 g of glaze—enough to dip the pieces into (see *Weighing and mixing*, page 8).
- Holding the sides of each piece, dip face down into the glaze, ensuring that glaze covers the entire piece, even the legs.
- Remove from the glaze bucket and hold vertically to allow excess glaze to drip back into the bucket.
- Wipe any glaze off the waxed areas of the feet.
- Place on a board and allow to dry.
- Repeat this procedure until all pieces have been glazed.
- Finally, apply a mixture of clear glaze plus a blue stain, or the brushwork blue recipe on page 60, on a loaded brush. (You might like to practise first on newspaper to achieve a steadiness of line.) Once the brushwork decoration is complete, handle as little as possible to prevent smudging.

To load and fire

Load all pieces in the usual way in an electric kiln.

- Fire terracotta, slip-decorated pieces without a clear glaze to 1040–1080°C.
- Fire white earthenware, underglaze-decorated pieces with clear earthenware glaze to the temperature recommended in the recipe for your choice of clear glaze.
- Fire zircon white-glazed, woven-coil pieces with blue brushwork decoration to 1120°C with a *soak* at maturing temperature.

© **3** *Decorative Spoons*
Ⓑ
Ⓐ
This project introduces you to the skill of pinching clay to create ceramic spoon forms, to which you add coil handles. Different textures of clay demonstrate constrasting surface qualities from fine white porcelain to coarse textured stoneware.

Materials

Feeneys red raku (earthenware clay) or Feeneys BRT clay (stoneware clay)
Clayworks SWS porcelain (or any porcelain clay)
White and coloured slips
Black stain
Underglaze colours.

Collect and observe the different types of spoons around you—ladles, scoops, wooden spoons all offer different interpretations.

To pinch bowls

- Start with small amounts of clay. Balls about 2–5 cm in diameter will allow you to create small shallow bowls that will form the main part of the spoon.
- Pinch by pressing gently and turning (see *Pinching*, page 17). Experiment with different spoon forms—they can vary greatly in shape from the shovel style to the scoop style.
- Once you have pinched a number of base forms, allow them to set up briefly.

- Refine them by trimming the edges, smoothing out bumps, etc.
- Cover in light plastic and leave while you are making the handle part of the spoon.

To form coil handles

Many types of handles can be made for the spoons. Coils may be rolled, then flattened, curved or angled, and can be given texture by being rolled on a patterned surface or paddled with a textured paddle.

To create a spiral effect on soft coils, gently press and roll the edge of a ruler along the coil a 45° angle. You'll find the coil rotates under the ruler as you do this. To create an impressed ridge, roll the ruler at a right angle to the coil.

- Roll a number of coils of varying lengths and diameters, in proportion to the size of the spoon bowls you have made.
- Texture them as you wish and shape into handles.
- You might wish to model the tops of the handles into small creatures or birds, or use coils to form interesting shapes. Remember, the spoons are decorative rather than functional, so your creative scope is unlimited!

To join handles to bowls

- Slice the bottom 2 cm of the coil handle lengthwise in half to divide the coil. This will enable you to attach the coil both front and back to the bowl of the spoon.

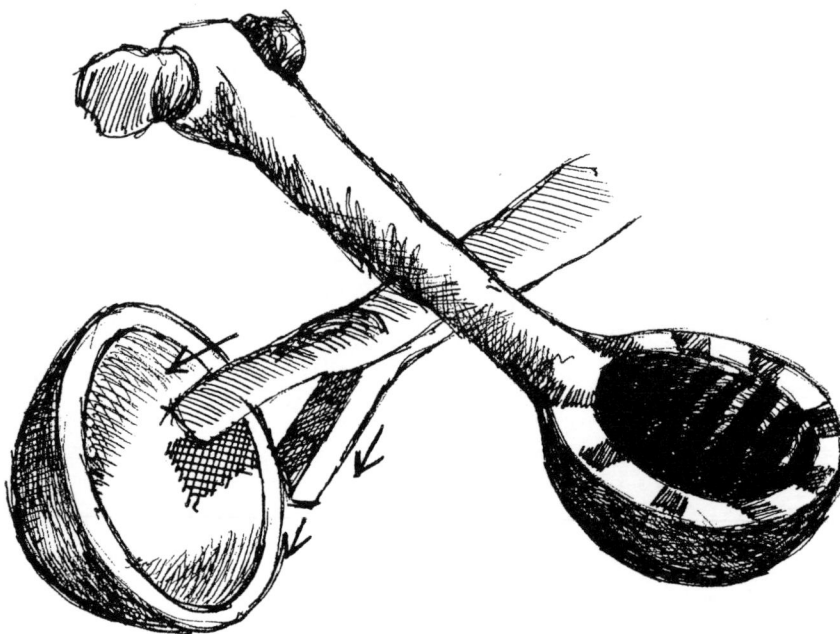

Joining the handle to the spoon

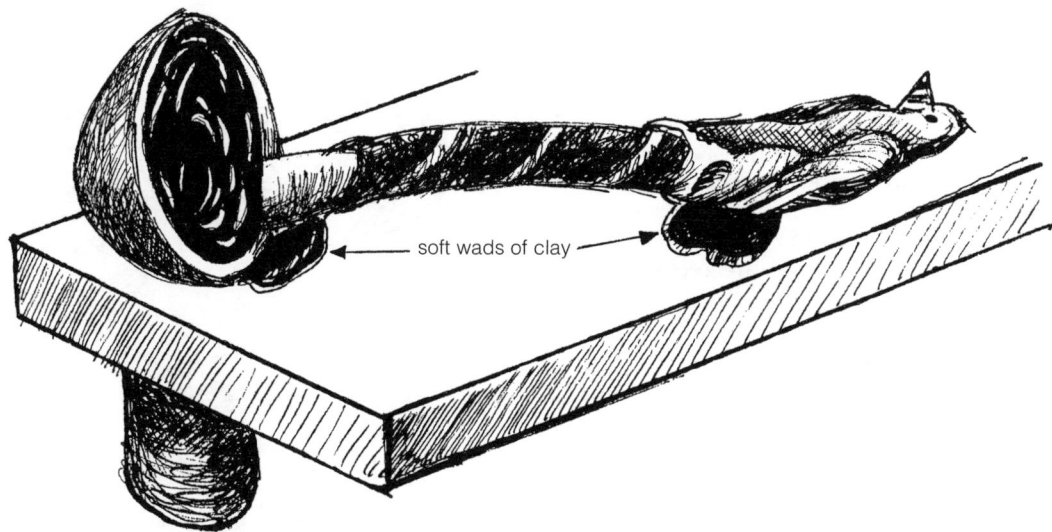

Wads of clay are used to prevent glazed parts sticking to the kiln shelf

- Score the surface of the bowl front and back where the coil is to join, and paint slip on. Place the coil handle on the spoon bowl front and back so that the spoon bowl is sandwiched between the two halves.
- Squeeze the coil and flatten both front and back to join the handle to the bowl of the spoon. Ensure that no air is trapped in the joins.
- Lay the spoon on a flat, absorbent surface and gently smooth the joined coil to the spoon bowl, using a small wooden tool. The handle and bowl of the spoon should now appear as one piece. You may need to add a small ball of clay on either side of the coil handle where it joins the spoon bowl to strengthen this area.
- If necessary, adjust the angle of the spoon bowl and curve the handle by placing a piece of wooden dowel (2 cm diameter) or some foam under the curve of the handle and in front of the spoon bowl for support until the clay has set up.
- Allow the spoons to set to leatherhard stage.
- Clean the spoons up. If you wish, you can carve detail into the spoon.
- Allow spoons to dry fully. Sand lightly if you want smooth surfaces to paint on. Handle carefully at this stage as the pieces will be very fragile—if possible, support each piece on a piece of foam while sanding and use a minimum of pressure. Remember—there is no need to sand if you want to maintain a rustic effect.

To decorate

- Using a damp sponge, lightly sponge each piece to remove any clay dust.
- Decorate spoons made of the red raku or stoneware textured clay by painting with coloured slips (see page 23). Use a limited range of

colours—a light, medium and dark colour will provide contrast. You can achieve a bold, lively surface by painting on the solid colour areas first, allowing these to dry, then overpainting the detail—lines, dots, etc.
- Paint the porcelain or finer white clay spoons with slips or underglazes. Consider your design carefully because later, after the bisque firing, you'll put clear glaze on top of the painted underglaze. Underglaze and slip do not stick to kiln shelves but glaze does.

To bisque

- Bisque-fire the porcelain spoons in an electric kiln to 1000°C, handling carefully so as to avoid smearing the underglaze.

To glaze

- Wax the areas of the spoon that will be in contact with the kiln shelf (spoon back and tip of handle) before glazing.
- Apply a clear commercial glaze such as CMG-100 to the underglaze-decorated porcelain spoons by dipping the spoon into the glaze, holding the top of the handle.
- Touch up any missed areas with a brush.
- Allow to dry.

To load and fire

- Load glazed porcelain spoons so that they are not touching, supported by wads attached to unglazed areas.
- The porcelain spoons are fired to 1220°C.
- The red raku or stoneware, slip-decorated pieces may be single-fired at temperatures ranging from 1060–1220°C, depending on how dark you wish the colours to be (the higher the temperature the darker the slips).

Ⓒ
Ⓑ
Ⓐ

4 Set of Pinched Cups

This project will help you develop the skill of pinching clay—a useful, direct and expressive way in which to work with clay. Colouring clay as a method of decoration is also explored. Your set of cups might comprise two, or ten if you are feeling ambitious.

Materials

A white, high-firing clay, such as porcelain or porcelaineous-stoneware, that responds well to colourants (I used RVC from Clayworks—see *Suppliers*, page 61).

!
CAUTION

To colour the clay

- Colour your clay with stains (see *Colouring Clay*, page 22). Two colours of high contrast will give you a definite pattern. I used a black, white and grey colour scheme.
- If colouring ahead of time, wrap up the clay until you are ready to use it.

To prepare the neriage block

- Roll the coloured clay into slabs 2.5 mm thick, approximately 50 mm by 150 mm.
- Layer the slabs alternately to create a striped effect, following the instructions for neriage on page 24. You may vary the thickness of the neriage block—up to 30 mm is sufficient.
- Wrap in plastic.

To prepare balls of clay for pinching

- Weigh out a number of equal pieces of clay— 100 g is a comfortable size to start with. Wrap in plastic.

To incorporate the neriage layer into the balls, choose one of the two methods described on page 24.

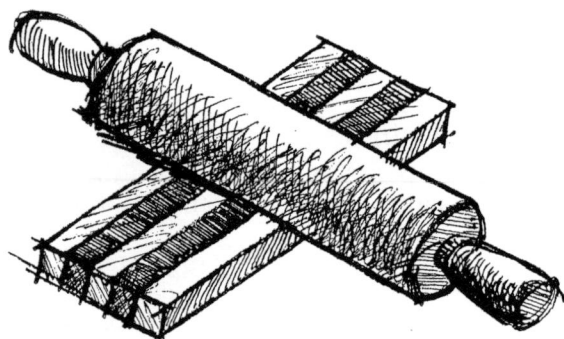

Flattening a slice off the neriage block

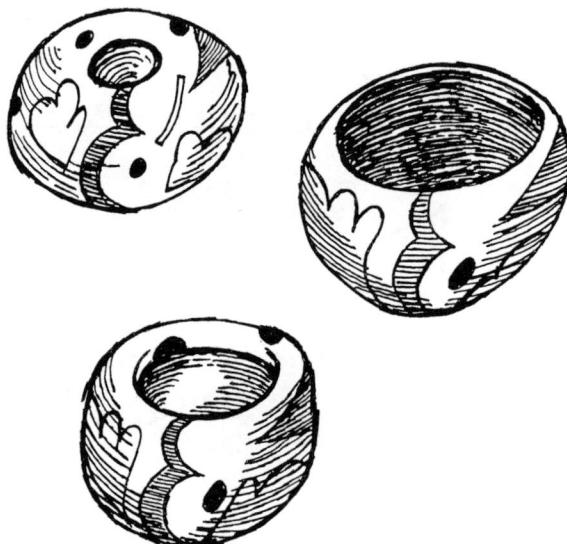

- You may vary where you place your opening hole in relation to the neriage layer, in order to change the position of the pattern on the finished cup.
- To increase the number of possible patterns, cut slices off the neriage block, roll them out and cut in halves or triangles, or join them together. Place these pieces onto the outside of the ball and roll smooth again. When pinched into forms these patterns will occur only on the outside of the cup; the inside will remain unpatterned.
- Create simple striped effects by cutting a slice off the neriage block, flattening with a rolling pin and laying the stripes on the side of the ball, ready to pinch.

Before pinching, determine whether you wish your cups to have straight or rounded sides.

To pinch the cups

- Pinch each of the balls carefully into a cup form (see *Pinching*, page 17). You can use a paddle to keep the sides straight. Support the cups in plastic cups or small bisque bowls (pukis) to stiffen up. (This prevents the bottom from flattening and the shape from distorting.)

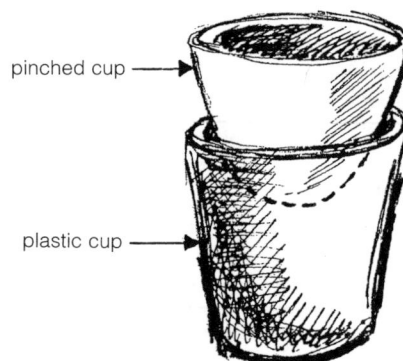

pinched cup ⟶

plastic cup ⟶

To pinch the bases

- While the cups are stiffening, pinch very shallow disc forms which will be the convex bases for the cups. If you wish, you can make these in coloured clay to contrast with the cup.

pinched cup base

- Check that the discs sit flat when inverted, to provide a stable base for the cup. Allow to stiffen to leatherhard.

The rims of the cups will be irregular from pinching. If you wish to make them even, you can trim them with scissors at the leatherhard stage.

When both cups and bases are leatherhard, they are ready to be joined together.

To join cups and bases

- Prepare a slurry (see page 18), using vinegar instead of water—this will prevent the layers of coloured clay from separating.
- Roughen the bottom of the cup and the top of the disc where they will join by cross-hatching with a pin tool. Paint slurry on both surfaces and press gently together. The safest way to do this is to place the cup rim-down and add the disc base to the cup.
- Once the cup has set up, turn right side up and adjust to make sure the cup sits straight on the disc.
- Wrap loosely in plastic to allow cups to dry slowly.

To finish and decorate

- Lightly sand each cup (wear a mask), to smooth the surfaces and even out any bumps. Sanding the rim of the cup will round it off, making it more comfortable to drink from.

If you choose to sand on a pad of foam, remove dust from foam regularly—don't allow it to accumulate. Wash the foam pad often to keep it clean but don't rest your work on wet foam.

- Brush away excess clay, then use a metal kidney to scrape the surface (this clarifies the pattern).
- If you wish, you can decorate the cups further using underglaze mixed with medium and painted on the pieces. (I painted the insides of the cups with underglaze colour, making sure not to over-saturate the cup and thus risk cracking it apart.)

To bisque

- Bisque-fire in an electric kiln to 1000°C.

To glaze

- Use a clear stoneware glaze or a commercial clear such as CMG-100.
- Pour glaze inside cups, quickly tip out excess. Allow to dry.
- To glaze the outside of the cups, turn upside-down. Holding the base, quickly dip into glaze bucket. Allow to drain, then clean unwanted glaze from areas such as base.
- Allow to dry.

To load and fire

- Make sure kiln shelves are flat and have a good coating of kiln wash (see page 60).
- Load, and fire slowly to 1220°C.

Ⓒ
Ⓑ
Ⓐ

5 Candlesticks

This project explores slab, pinch and coil techniques in combination. By joining bowl, cone and cylinder forms, you will be able to produce balanced, expressive forms for holding candles.

Materials

Terracotta earthenware
White earthenware clay
Curved *formers* (bisque) to shape candlestick base.

To form the base

Each candlestick consists of a base, a stem (formed from a cylinder) and a cup. You can also add branches (or arms) with joiners, and handles.
- Roll out flat slabs of clay 8 mm thick. Using a cup or a small bowl as a cutting guide, cut circles about 100 mm in diameter from the slabs.
- Lay each circle *on top* of a curved former.
- Make a number of bases of varying sizes and lay on formers to set up.

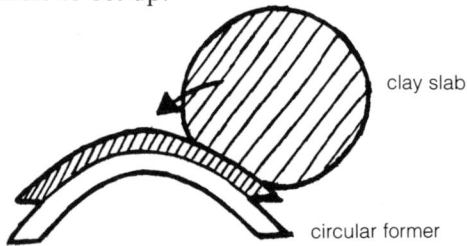

clay slab

circular former

To form the stem and arms

- Roll out a number of fat coils of different lengths and thicknesses. For the base stem you will need a thickness of 30 mm. For the branches (or arms) you will need narrower cylinders. You should work from a wide base (for stability) and reduce the diameter of the cylinders as you build up the candlestick (for structural strength).
- Insert a bamboo skewer along the length of each cylinder to form a tube. Ensure that the skewer goes right through the middle of the cylinder, end to end.
- Roll the cylinder on a flat surface with the skewer inside to enlarge the hole. You may use a knitting needle or a fatter skewer to make the tube hole bigger—8–10 mm is a good size for the opening. If you wish the cylinder to be wider on one end, roll this end for longer than the other end.

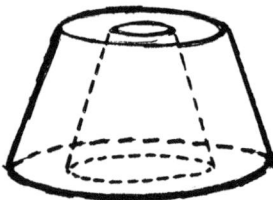

Cylinder shape may be wider at one end

- If you wish, you can texture the outside of these cylinders by rolling on a textured surface. Ridges and indentations can be made in the surface of the cylinder by rolling it along the length of a bamboo skewer or running the edge of a ruler diagonally around the cylinder to create an indentation.
- Wrap in plastic until ready to assemble.

To form joiners

- Roll balls of clay (like large beads) of varying sizes. Flatten into discs and carefully cut holes in the centres. These discs will act as joiners between the cylinders.

Joiners

To form joining and stabilising coils

- Roll smaller coils of clay—8–12 mm thick by 200 mm long. (These will be useful to strengthen joins, to create handles, or to bridge candlesticks with more than one stem.)
- Wrap in plastic ready for assembling.

To form the cup

- Pinch out a small ball of clay into a cup form (see *Pinching*, page 17).
- Place a small ringed coil inside the cup (this will help steady the candle). Have a candle available, and check the diameter to ensure a proper fit. Remember, clay shrinks during drying and firing, so make the cup that holds the candle slightly larger. Cut a small hole in the bottom of the cup.

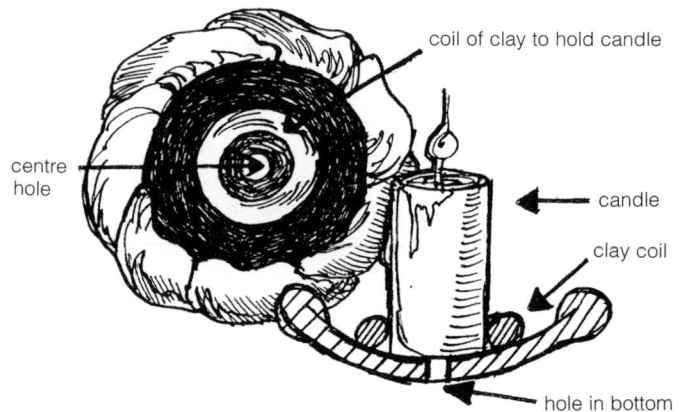

coil of clay to hold candle

centre hole

candle

clay coil

hole in bottom

To assemble

- Make up a slurry, using vinegar instead of water.
- Leaving each slab base (which should have stiffened nicely) on its bisque formers, score the surface of the base and paint the clay slurry on.
- Select one of the fattest cylinders for the stem of the candlestick, and paint slurry on the bottom.
- Join the cylinder to the centre of the slab base. Paddle the top of the cylinder to ensure a good join.
- Run a small coil of clay around the join—press and smooth into place to further secure the join.
- Score the top of the cylinder and a joiner, paint both surfaces with slurry, press and paddle together.

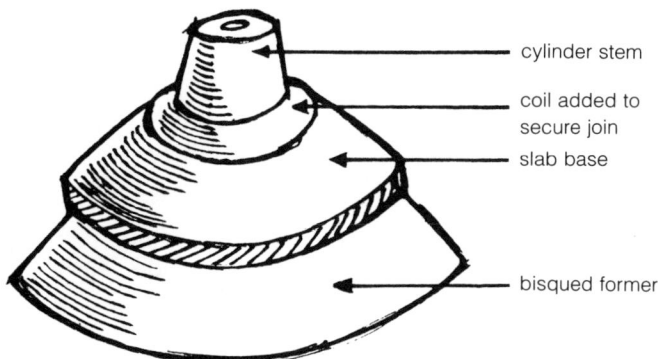

Candlestick components

cylinder stem
coil added to secure join
slab base
bisqued former

To decorate

- Sponge candlesticks lightly before painting to remove dust.
- Paint white earthenware candlesticks with underglaze.
- If you wish, experiment with wax resist (see page 23), perhaps using the technique to apply layers of colour.
- Paint terracotta candlesticks with white or coloured slips. If you sgraffito lines into the clay while it is still wet, these lines may be filled with copper oxide or carbonate using a paintbrush, then sponged back to remove excess copper, leaving only the copper in the lines. This will emphasise the lines, coloured slip may then be painted on, avoiding the coppered lines.

!
CAUTION

To bisque

- Bisque-fire the white earthenware in an electric kiln to 1000°C.

To glaze, load and fire

- Glaze white earthenware candlesticks with a clear glaze and fire in an electric kiln to 1120°C.
- Single-fire slip-decorated terracotta unglazed candlesticks in an electric kiln to 1060–1120°C (the higher the temperature, the darker the terracotta). Alternatively, you may wish to experiment with clear-glazing the coloured areas of the terracotta-slip decorated candlesticks to provide a contrast between shiny and matt surfaces.

Note: Glazed pieces are easier to clean!

You can add cylinders, coils and joiners in a variety of ways to form differently shaped candlesticks (or candelabras!) Be patient: allow each section to stiffen—use a heat gun or a hair dryer to stiffen each section joined to base before adding the next. It is useful to work on two or three candlesticks at the same time. This allows each to set up while you work on the other.

- When you have achieved the height you desire, place the cup on top, scoring, slurrying, pressing and paddling as before.

You can build candlesticks of many different sizes and shapes—even multi-armed, as long as the base is wide enough to support the superstructure. Additions such as handles or small birds and animals can be incorporated to give a humorous or personal style to the candlestick.

Remember, *visual* and *physical* balance are important.

- Once you have assembled all the parts, wrap in plastic and allow to dry very slowly so that joins do not pull apart and to prevent warping.

Different cup shapes

Ⓒ
Ⓑ # 6 Fish Dishes
Ⓐ

This project explores the use of evenly rolled slabs of clay which are draped on top of or laid inside a former to create various types of flatware.

Materials

Terracotta earthenware clay
White earthenware clay
Formers— to make formers you'll need sheets of 25 mm-thick rigid styrofoam (obtainable from a sign-writing supply shop or building suppliers), PVA glue, metal ruler, matt knife, black felt pen, rough- and fine-grade sandpaper, bread knife to cut styrofoam.

To form the dish

- Make a positive or a negative former (see page 19).
- Roll slabs of clay of even thickness (about 10 mm) to a size that will cover the length and width of your former. Allow at least 20 cm extra around the outside—this will provide a flat rim for decorating.
- Gently lay the soft slab of clay into the negative former, or over the positive former. Using a damp sponge, ease the clay against the shape. You can use a rubber kidney to smooth the clay.
- Trim excess clay and round edges by sponging.
- Allow clay to set up until it is stiff enough to remove from the former. If you place a board on top of the shape, then flip it, the fish dish should pop out easily onto the board.
- Be careful when draping clay over a positive former—as clay dries it will shrink and tighten onto the form, making it difficult to remove. If left too long on the former it will crack, so check regularly.
- Allow forms to stiffen to leatherhard stage then refine the shape with a metal scraper. Allow to dry fully.
- Lightly sand and sponge if necessary.

To decorate

- Paint red terracotta clay with white slip at leather-hard stage. (This will provide a white background for the blue decoration.) Allow slip to dry.
- Decorate with brushwork blue pigment of water-colour consistency (see page 60).

You can use wax resist in some places to block out areas that you want to keep white. To get a darker or more opaque blue, lay in some blue brushwork decoration, sgraffito through to the red clay, then paint wax resist on and place another coat of blue pigment in some areas.

Many patterns and effects may be obtained by playing with these three elements—brush marks, sgraffito, and wax resist.

To bisque

- Bisque-fire terracotta and white earthenware pieces in an electric kiln to 1000°C.

To glaze

Note: The pouring method will work best with this type of form.

- Glaze terracotta slip pieces using earthenware clear glaze (see page 60) or commercial clear CEG-01. First pour onto inside and allow to dry, then glaze outside of dish. Wash off excess glaze from bottom. Allow to dry.
- Glaze white earthenware pieces zircon white, first inside the piece (allow to dry), then outside. Wash off excess glaze on bottom.
- Decorate pieces on top of white glaze using a small amount of the glaze mixed into the brushwork blue pigment. Allow to dry.

To load and fire

- Load decorated, glazed pieces onto clean kiln shelves and ensure that the pieces do not touch each other.
- Fire clear-glazed pieces in an electric kiln to 1120°C.
- Fire zircon-white-glazed pieces in an electric kiln to 1120–1160°C.

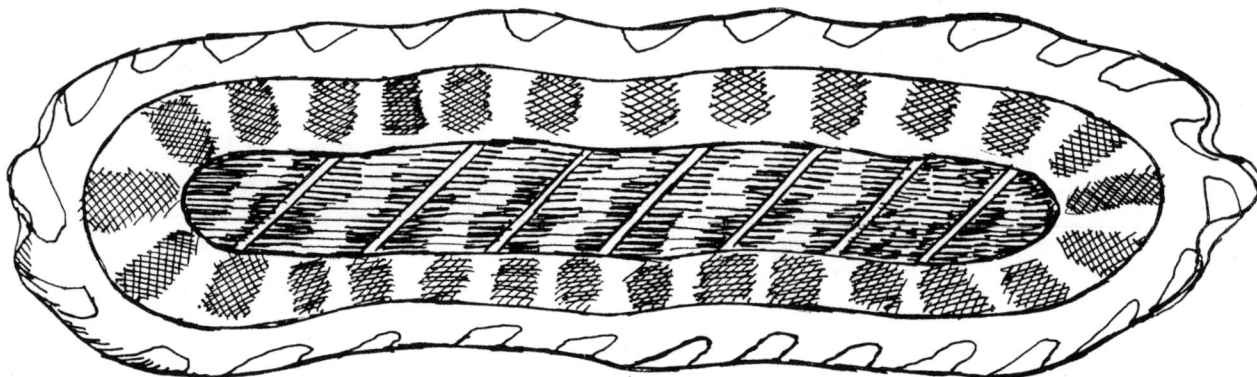

Decorated fish dish

Ⓒ
Ⓑ # 7 *Bowls*
Ⓐ

Bowls are a fundamental ceramic form with many applications as a container for daily use in the kitchen: fruit and salad bowls, bowls for pasta, rice, soup, desserts, porridge and pudding—each has a form suited to the food it will contain. This project explores the bowl in its variety of forms using the slab and coil–pinch methods.

Materials

White stoneware clay (I used JB.3 from Clayworks)
A pencil
Fine steel wool
A chamois or a soft piece of leather
A banding wheel or turning wheel (useful for turning coiled forms easily).

Study the shapes of a variety of bowls—you will notice that they have a curved belly which flares out or encloses, and they have a rim, lip or flange, and a foot. By replicating such shapes you can create beautiful bowls, as large as you like.

If you work on more than one bowl at a time, you can add a coil to the next bowl while waiting for the last one to stiffen.

To form the base

- Roll out a slab of clay 8–10 mm thick, and lay it inside a puki, or bowl form. This will be the curved belly of your bowl.
- Cover with plastic.

Puki or bowl former

To roll the coils

- Roll a number of coils of even diameter and store in plastic. The optimum diameter of the coils will be determined by the size of the bowl you wish to make. For a small bowl, coils should be about 1 cm thick; for a medium bowl, about 1.5 cm thick; and for a large bowl (salad or fruit), about 2 cm.

To add coils to base

- Cut the first coil long enough to go around the top of the slab base. Place on top, slightly to the inside.
- Join the coil to the inside of the bowl by smearing the soft clay down onto the slab with your fingers. Repeat on the outside of the coil. Joining the first coil on the outside is the most difficult because you need to tilt the slab out of the puki in order to smear the coil onto the outer wall.
- Having smeared and joined both sides of the coil to the clay slab, use your wooden tool to work over the smeared clay and further join it to the base slab. Use a wooden rib to smooth, then paddle the join. When paddling, hold one hand inside the pot for support while using the wooden paddle on the outer wall.
- Thin out and heighten the coil, by pinching it all around with your thumb and first finger. Paddle again.

Thinning coils

- Repeat the above procedure (add coil, smear inside and out, work with wooden tool, smooth with rib, paddle, pinch, paddle, allow to stiffen) until you have added sufficient coils.

To form the rim

- Finish off with a slightly thicker coil, and leave it rounded or paddle it flat.
- Give the bowl a straight, even top by trimming the coil with a knife or create a wide, flat or angled rim by pinching the coil out.

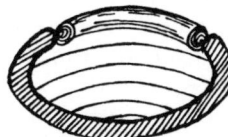

add coil to inside edge of previous coil to make bowl curve inward

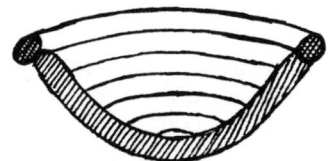

add coil to outside edge of previous coil to make bowl flare out

Shaping the bowl

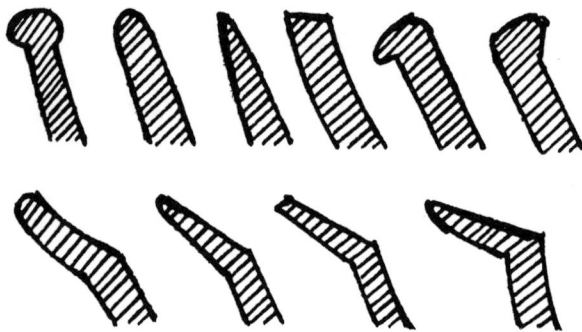

Different rim profiles

- Smooth the rim by applying a chamois, a damp-ened piece of soft leather or a sponge while turning the bowl full circle.

To finish

- Leaving the bowl inside its former, wrap it loosely in plastic and uncover it for increasing lengths of time until it has set to leatherhard stage.
- When the bowl is ready to be removed from the bisque puki it should pull away easily. It will feel stiff and slightly rubbery, but not dry.
- Handling carefully, give it a final paddle to consolidate the form.

To add the foot

Turn the bowl upside-down and place on top of your puki or a piece of foam to avoid damage to the rim.

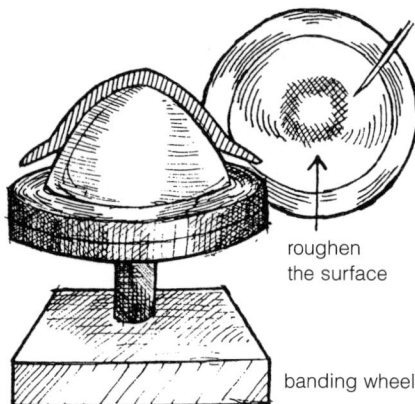

Attaching the foot

- Place the bowl on the banding wheel and, using a bamboo skewer, score a light line on the base where you want the foot to be.
- Roughen the surface where the coil will be attached to the bottom of the bowl, add slip, then press the coil into place.
- Join the coil to the base of the bowl inside and outside, turning the banding wheel as you go. A higher foot or one that flares out will require more coils.
- Smooth foot and allow to set up to leatherhard.

While a foot is not absolutely necessary, it does lift the bowl form and improve its shape. It also makes glazing easier and, if it flares out, can give the bowl extra stability.

To dry and finish

- Allow the bowls to dry to leatherhard, then scrape back with a metal scraper to smooth out bumps and dints and 'find the form' or refine the shape.
- Once dry, bowls may be further refined by sanding.

To decorate

- Paint a variety of coloured slips onto the raw clay, and sgraffito through the slips to create a white outline. Or:
- If you prefer a black outline, draw lines into leatherhard clay with a bamboo skewer, then fill with black slip using a brush. When the bowl is dry use a metal scraper to scrape the excess black slip away, leaving a clean black line. Then paint coloured slips inside the shape created by the black outline. Or:
- Create a 'scumbled' effect by layering different colours of slip on top of one another with a paintbrush, allowing it to dry then scratching back using steel wool to scratch through and show contrasting colours underneath. Wear a mask and work in a well-ventilated area.

Patterns such as lines and dots can be created by painting on slip of one colour, allowing it to dry, then painting the pattern on top with another colour of slip. Images of fruit, flowers, animals, etc., or patterns, may be drawn on top of the coloured slip lightly in pencil, then painted in with contrasting slip colours. To add further detail or create a watercolour wash effect over the slip, paint on underglaze mixed with medium.

To bisque

- Bisque-fire decorated pieces to 1000°C.

To glaze

Glaze with commercial clear stoneware glaze CMG-100 or earthenware clear gloss (see page 60) and load.

To load and fire

- Fire stoneware-glazed bowls in an electric or a gas kiln to 1220°C.
- Fire earthenware-glazed bowls to 1060–1260°C.

!
CAUTION

© Ⓑ Ⓐ 8 Spice Containers

In this project a solid piece of clay is shaped into a form, then carved out to create the hollow inside of the container. Surface qualities are applied to the solid form before it is hollowed out. (See *Hollowing Out*, page 20.) This method enables you to approach form in a free and expressive manner.

Materials

Earthenware white clay or terracotta, providing neither is 'groggy'. Avoid coarse clays as they make carving out difficult. A light or white clay works well with stains and slips, or underglazes. Terracotta clay works well with coloured slips.

To form the containers

- Divide wedged clay into 5 or 6 balls of similar size.
- Roll clay on the work table and paddle or shape in your hands until you have achieved the desired form for your spice containers (round, cubic, cylindrical, pyramid shape, etc.).
- Form all your balls of clay similarly, line them up and allow to set up slightly. If you wish to texture the forms, do so at this stage.

To form feet and knobs

- Roll small balls of clay, then shape them.

Many different types of feet and knobs are possible, but it is important to relate the styles to each other. For the spice containers (pictured on the front and opposite page 16), I made little cones; coils may also be used. You can add texture by rolling the coils onto a textured surface before attaching. Feet and knobs, while not necessary, give the container character. And remember: three feet are more stable than four because it's much easier to get three feet to stand evenly.

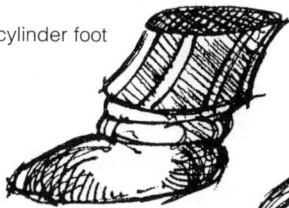
cylinder foot

coil foot

cone foot

Assorted shapes for feet

position of feet

Attach feet before hollowing out

To attach feet and knobs

- Score the surface of the bottom of the container where you wish the feet to be, paint on slip, then join. Press onto container firmly.
- Press the container lightly onto the flat work surface to make the feet level.
  Note: Feet are added in a triangular arrangement onto the bottom of the container *before* it is hollowed out or decorated.
- Using the same joining method, add the knobs to the top of the container form.
- Cover pieces loosely with plastic so they do not dry out too much. Allow pieces to set up overnight.

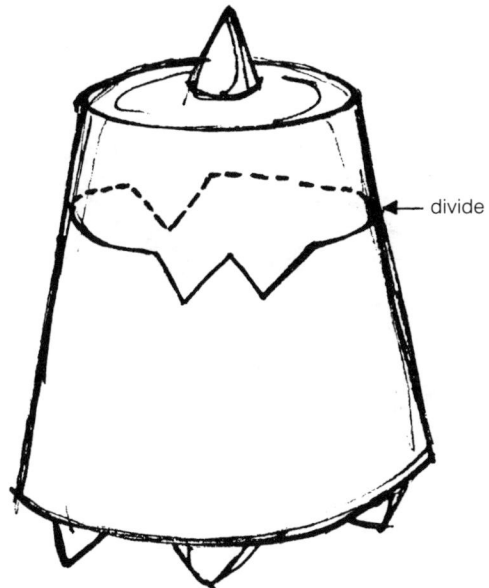
← divide

To separate the lid from the container form

- Using your pin tool or bamboo skewer, lightly draw a line around each container, approximately three quarters of the way up, to divide the top from the bottom. This line must have curves or angles in it to key the lid snugly into the body of the container and prevent it from sliding off sideways.
- With your clay knife, make one cut into the centre

of the container from the side; then, carefully following the drawn line, move the knife around the line, keeping the tip of your knife in the centre, until the top piece is separate from the bottom. Repeat for all containers.

To hollow out the forms

Begin with the lids of the spice containers. Using the bamboo skewer, draw a line on the underside of the top about 8–10 mm from the edge. This marks the width of the wall, acting as a guide for hollowing out.

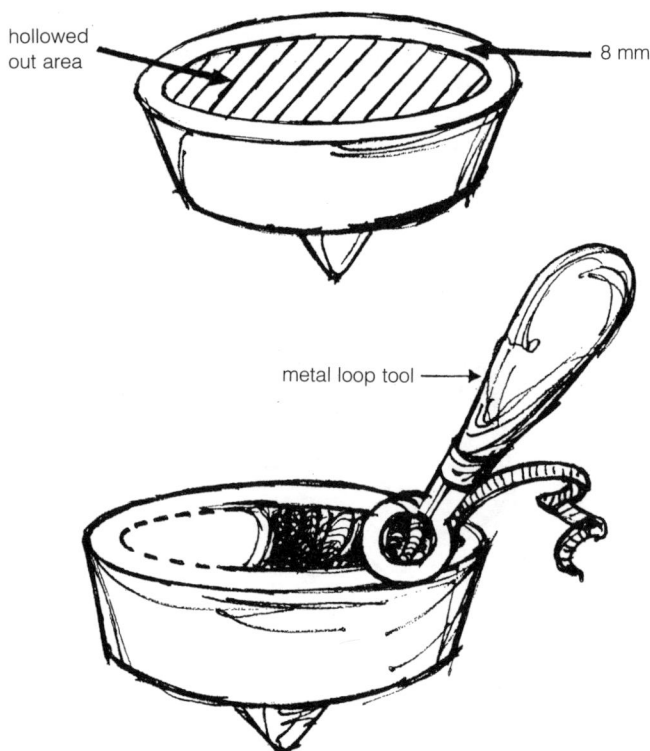

Hollowing out spice container lid

- Using your small metal loop tool, carefully begin scooping out the clay inside the line you have drawn. Scoop out small amounts of clay evenly all over to ensure that you do not go wider than the 8 mm. If the clay is too soft and the lid starts to distort, allow it to set up more before continuing.
- Hollow the container bottoms out in the same manner. Since they are deeper, you will need to be careful, when approaching the bottom, not to allow the base of the container to become thinner than the walls. Both base and walls should be of equal width to allow for even shrinkage and avoid cracking.
- Allow each piece to set up before giving the inside a final scraping to smooth it.

To finish

- Test the lid on each container to ensure a snug fit. Smooth the edges of the lids and container tops by scraping lightly—but do not take away too much clay, or the lids will not fit properly.
- Allow containers to dry (with lids in place) to leatherhard stage.
- Sgraffito lines using a bamboo skewer to create patterns or divisions of space. You can write the names of spices on the lids at this stage.
- Allow pieces to dry fully.
- Sand the *insides* of the forms carefully with steel wool to smooth further.

To decorate

- Lightly sponge to remove dust, then use a brush to paint the sgraffitoed lines with a mixture of black copper oxide and water.
- Allow to dry, then sponge surface to remove excess oxide. Black copper oxide should remain in the lines, delineating the patterns or textures you have made.
- Paint the spice containers with your choice of coloured slips. Simple, bold patterns that follow the form will work best. Colours should harmonise, so test before deciding on your final colour combinations.
- Allow to dry fully.

To bisque

- Bisque-fire to 1000°C.

To glaze and fire

- Glaze the *inside* only, avoiding the edges where the lid and bottom meet, or they will stick together.
- Glaze fire to the temperature recommended for the clear earthenware glaze you are using.

Ⓘ
Ⓐ

9 *Commemorative Serving Platter*

Using slabs of even thickness draped over formers, this project enables you to create a ceramic 'canvas' on which images and designs may be painted, and messages written to celebrate a memorable occasion.

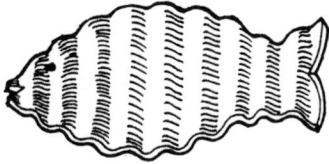

Materials

White earthenware clay (I used SWE from Clayworks, but any white-firing clay, including stoneware or porcelain, would be suitable, providing you use the appropriate glaze and test the colours at the chosen firing temperature before beginning to paint.)
Found objects—these can be utilised as formers for the serving platters (I used a piece of corrugated iron to create the 'waves' for the 'Chris Catches His First Fish' platter, and a piece of craftwood cut into an oval for the 'Nyssa is 10' platter.)

Platters may be made in a variety of shapes: rectangular, oval or circular. You may wish to be more expressive and make the platter in the shape of an animal, or a fruit, vegetable or fish. There is plenty of inspiration in nature to give you fresh ideas. Let the event you wish to celebrate be a guide to the shape and decoration you might use.

To roll the slabs

- Roll out a slab of clay of even thickness (about 8–10 mm), the size you require. You may need to roll out two slabs and join them to obtain the required size. Join thoroughly, then roll over the join again with the rolling pin to prevent splitting during drying or firing.
- Cover slab loosely with plastic.

To prepare formers

- Cover your formers with strips of damp newspaper to prevent sticking. Sponge newspaper with water, wiping excess away before laying the slab of clay on top.

To form the platter

- Cut the slab of clay to the approximate shape you require and lay carefully on the former. A piece of light canvas laid under the slab before cutting will allow you to transfer it to the former without stretching or breaking it.
- Using a damp sponge and a rubber kidney, gently smooth and firmly press the clay, going over the clay slab until you are satisfied it has taken on the required shape.

- Allow the slab to set up on the former (either uncovered for a few hours, or lightly covered overnight), then trim the edges with a clay knife. If you wish, you may add handles at this stage.
- Using wooden tools or ribs give the clay a final shaping.
- Dry the piece slowly and carefully. The larger the piece, the longer the drying time required.

To decorate

- Place your platter on a flat board to prevent breakages and facilitate handling.
- Sand, and sponge lightly.
- Draw your chosen image or pattern onto the clay with a pencil. (You may find it helpful to draw the design or image on paper, and try out various colours first, to guide you before working on the clay surface.)
- Prepare your palette of underglaze colours mixed with medium. Colours of high contrast work best. Have clean water available to thin the colours further where necessary. Apply colour to all pencilled areas and allow to dry.
- Using a sgraffito tool, lightly carve through the underglaze to the white clay underneath. This results in a white outline to the painted patterns or images. Wear a mask to do this as it is dusty work. Use a dry paintbrush to dust the clay from the lines.
- Using a cotton bud, you may smudge areas of the painted underglaze to soften the colour or shade the area. This will give a muted effect.
- You can write messages by carving through the underglaze, or use a fine paintbrush to handpaint the message.

To bisque

- Bisque-fire in an electric kiln to 1000°C.

To glaze

- Clear glaze to bring out the underglaze designs. Use a thin consistency for optimum results. This can be brushed or poured on.

To load and fire

- Sprinkle freshly kiln-washed shelves lightly with grog or powdered alumina hydrate to prevent the platters from sticking and distorting.
- Fire slowly in an electric or gas kiln, to 1120°C for earthenware or 1120–1260°C for stoneware. A half-hour soak once the glaze has reached its maturing temperature will allow any pinholes to heal over and will give a smooth, buttery result.
- Cool slowly to prevent the glaze from crazing or the piece from cracking. Greater care is needed when you are working with large pieces of flat clay.

Projects for the Garden

ⓒ ⓑ ⓐ 10 Mini Herb Pots

This project combines several basic hand-building methods to create expressive, individual pots to grow herbs in. Modelling, and carving through slip provide simple methods of decoration without the use of glaze.

Materials

A rich coloured stoneware clay with an open textured body (I used Feeneys BRT—Feeneys red raku clay may be used if firing to earthenware temperature). White and black slip

To form the pots

- Divide wedged clay into balls the size of large oranges, or grapefruit size for a larger pot.
- Form the planters by patting the balls smooth, then rolling clay on the work table into a fat cylinder with the top slightly wider than the bottom. You may wish to make a more 'organic' form for the planter by shaping the ball into a sculptured form. Ensure you have a flattened base. Once pots are formed, allow to set up uncovered overnight.

To hollow out

- Using your bamboo skewer, draw a line on the top surface of the herb pot (the wider part), about 10 mm from the outside edge. This marks the width of the wall of your pot. Hollow out as for the spice containers (page 43), maintaining a wall thickness of 10 mm. (See also *Hollowing Out*, page 20.)

You can also form mini herb pots using pinching and coiling techniques (see pages 17 and 18). Coils should be about 15 mm diameter and should be added until the pot is about 120 mm high.

To model figures

- Using coils or balls of clay, you can make many imaginative figures or animals to attach to the top-edge of your pot. A bird's head or wings, leaves and flowers, fish and parrots are some ideas. Make them of a size that will match the pot, forming them before attaching to the pot. Allow them to set up slightly while attaching the feet.

To add feet

- Start with three fat cylinders, or flattened balls, of clay. Form feet in desired shapes. Attach and stabilise as for the spice containers. While it is not necessary to have feet on the herb pots, they can add character, particularly if they follow the theme of the modelled pieces you have made for the top.
- Join the modelled figures to the top rim; score the surface, paint on slurry and press on the figure.

To finish

- Wrap the pot in plastic and allow to dry to leather-hard stage.
- Further smooth and finish inside, decorate with painted slip and carving through slip on the outside. Cut a hole about 10 mm in diameter in the bottom of your pot to allow drainage.

To make saucers

- Make a saucer for the herb pot by rolling out a slab of clay 8–10 mm thick and draping it over a plaster or bisqued clay former. When stiffened, remove the clay from the former and add modelled figures to the rim, if you wish, to continue the theme of the pot.
- Allow to dry slowly on a flat board to prevent warping. Test the pot in the saucer to make certain it sits flat and doesn't wobble.

To make herb labels

- Roll small balls of clay and flatten them. Make coils of clay about 10 mm thick and 80 mm long. Taper one end. Join coils to the backs of the flattened balls by pressing into place and smoothing over.
- Using a ballpoint pen or a bamboo skewer, write the names of herbs on the front of the labels. Allow to dry slowly on a flat surface.
- When dry, paint copper oxide wash into the writing and sponge back. When fired, the written word will be black.

To decorate

- Decorate the pot and the saucer by painting with slip and carving through, as described on page 23.

To load and fire

- When dry, stack the herb pots, saucers and labels in the kiln (they will not stick). Single-fire, proceeding slowly (approximately 150°C per hour), to 1260°C in an electric kiln to achieve oxidation or to 1280°C in a gas kiln to achieve reduction. Stoneware clays are suitable for these temperatures.

⑪ *11 Bonsai Planter*

Ⓐ This project uses slab construction from cardboard templates, to translate two-dimensional shapes into three-dimensional, functional bonsai planters. Precision is required in the execution of this building technique. Slabs are assembled with box and mitre joints.

Materials

A rich-coloured stoneware clay with an open texture (I used Feeneys BRT, which fires well to mid-stoneware temperatures, and Feeneys red raku for earthenware firing.)
Shellac for washback technique
White and black slip

Designing shapes

To obtain ideas for the form of your bonsai planter, start by drawing two-dimensional shapes on paper. Brainstorm a variety of shapes by combining straight or curved lines and angles. These will be a starting point for your three-dimensional clay form.

When you have decided upon a suitable shape for the base, enlarge it by drawing on paper to the size you want your planter to be. Draw as accurately as possible. To draft the sides or walls of your planter, measure along the base shape on each of its sides, and draw the length of the base measurement for each of the sides on a piece of paper. You can determine the height of your planter, working to a minimum of approximately 7–9 cm. The walls will, of course, all be the same.

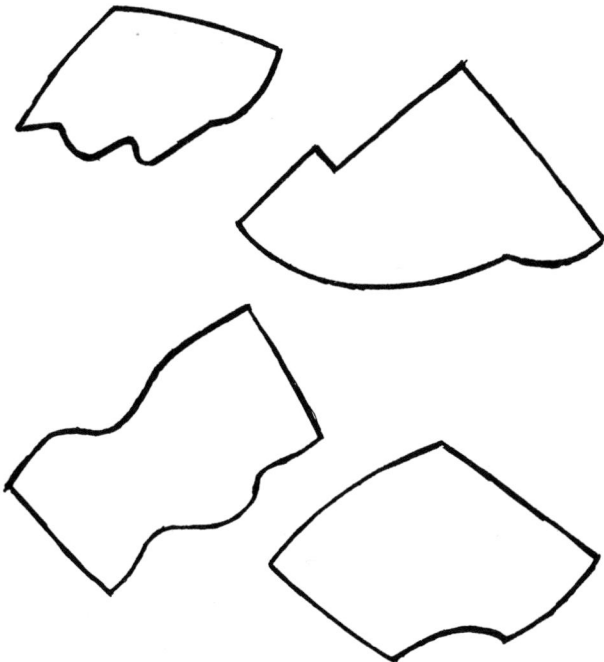

Ideas for base shapes

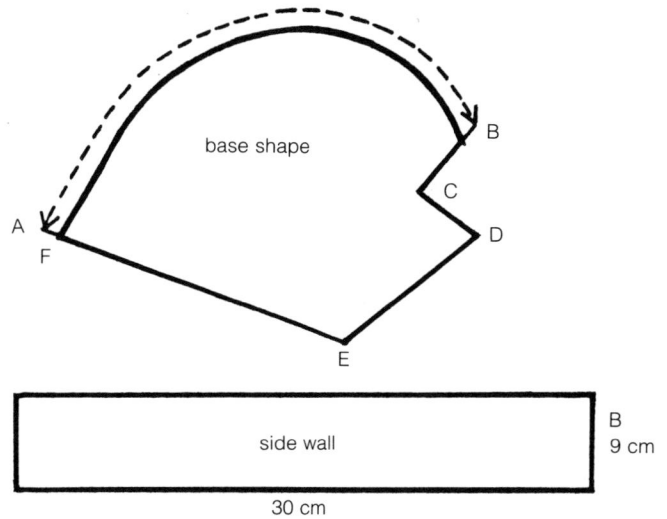

Measure distance from Side A–B and mark on template. Repeat for all sides of shape, e.g. B–C, C–D, D–E, E–F.

To make templates

• Test how the bonsai planter will look by cutting out the paper base and sides and taping together to create a three-dimensional model. Make the necessary adjustments. When you are satisfied with the results, accurately redraw the base and sides onto white card.
• Cut out carefully. Label all template pieces clearly.
• On the base card template, draw a line 10 mm inside the outer edge, all the way around the shape. This represents the thickness of the clay wall, and enables you to determine the angle at which it needs to be cut for a proper mitred joint.

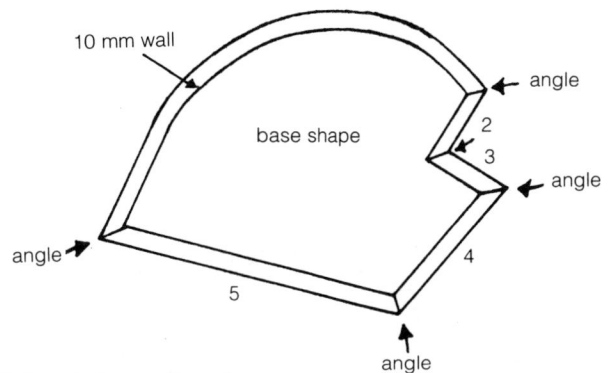

Determining wall angles

To roll slabs

• Roll out the number of slabs you will require to a thickness of 10 mm.
• Allow slabs to stiffen on cement sheeting, turn regularly for even drying. Slabs need to be stiff but still able to bend around curves without cracking.
• If you wish, you can impress texture into flat slabs while they are still soft, before stiffening and before cutting and assembling.

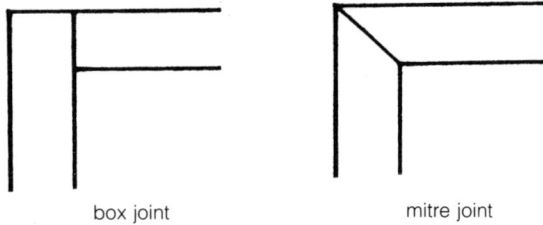

box joint   mitre joint

To cut slabs from templates

- Lay cardboard templates on the stiffened clay slabs and cut around the outer edge using a sharp clay knife. Make sure you cut straight down on the base shape.
- On the side templates, cut the bottom and top edges straight, but mitre the two ends to the correct angle as indicated on your base template.
- When all the clay pieces for the planter have been cut out, cover lightly with plastic, leaving the templates on top of the clay pieces for easy identification, until you are ready to assemble them.

To assemble

- Make up a slurry (see page 18), adding a small amount of vinegar to help prevent cracking along joins.
- Remove the template from the base piece, and lightly sketch a line 10 mm in from the outside edge (as done on template). Using a toothbrush or bamboo skewer, roughen the base where the side wall will join, and paint with slurry.
- Starting with your longest side wall, roughen and paint slurry on the bottom edge that will join to the base, place on the base and push firmly to join.
- Paint slurry over the join area, on base and wall, and lay a small coil of soft clay along the join. Using your finger, press into the join area and smooth over with a modelling tool.

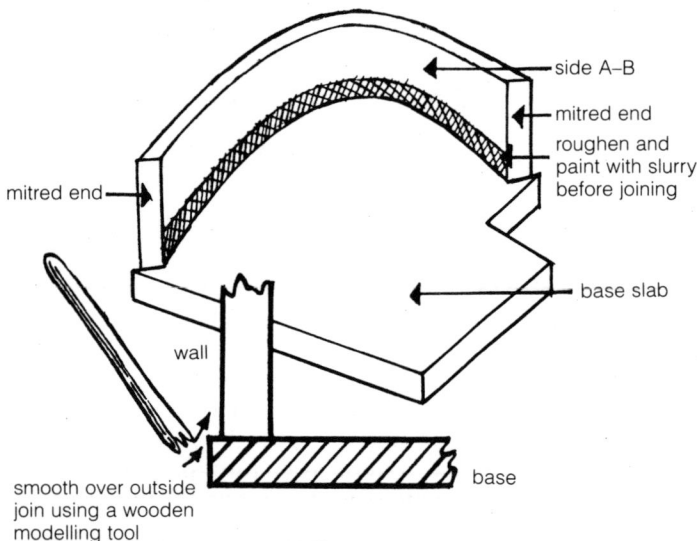

mitred end

side A–B

mitred end

roughen and paint with slurry before joining

base slab

wall

base

smooth over outside join using a wooden modelling tool

- Using your modelling tool, join base to outside of wall by dragging clay from the side of the base over the joined wall. Smooth with a rubber kidney.
- Add all sides in this manner until the pot is complete.
- Secure every join on the inside of the planter by adding a small coil of clay to each join and smoothing over. Further consolidate the joins by paddling lightly.
- Wrap piece in plastic and allow to set up.

To make a slab rim

- Using the base template as a guide, measure 5 mm on either side of the 10 mm wall. This will allow for a slab rim 20 mm wide (with an overhang of 5 mm each side of the wall).
- Cut a template for the rim, lay on a stiffened slab of clay and cut out. Allow to set up, then roughen and paint slurry on the underside of the slab rim, and the top edge of the walls. Carefully press rim into place. Paddle lightly, then cover in plastic.

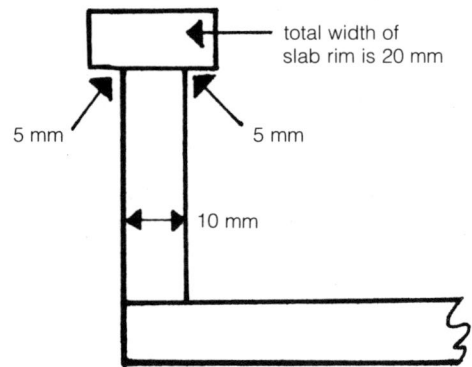

total width of slab rim is 20 mm

5 mm   5 mm

10 mm

To add slab feet

- Return to the original card template you made for the base to determine where your slab feet will be placed. Mark their position and length on the card and measure and cut slab pieces to fit. You may shape the slab feet in a variety of ways (see illustration).
- Position slab feet slightly in from the outside edge of the planter. The shape of the feet will depend on the shape of the base.
- Carefully turn planter onto its rim, mark location of the feet, roughen, paint slurry on both base and foot where they will join, and press into place. Smooth over join with a wooden tool.
- Wrap loosely in plastic and allow to dry slowly for a few days. Remove plastic and continue to dry until clay is warm to the touch (room temperature).

The shape of the fish dictates the dimensions these fish dishes take. Draped slabs of terracotta clay, painted with white slip and blue patterns give a warm pink/white effect. The white earthenware clay with white glaze and blue and yellow-painted decoration are much cooler-looking. Although fish dishes are ideal for serving fish, they are equally useful for hors-d'oeuvres, cheeses, a French stick or even a cake. The 'Pair of Pears' and 'Moe was a beautiful pig' spoon rests are practical as well as fun.

ABOVE: *This slab-built terracotta birdhouse can be hung by placing wooden dowels through the top three holes and attaching rope to the dowels. Alternatively, it looks equally attractive mounted on a tall post in the garden.*

The slip-decorated, coiled bowls and the hot plate stand are examples of how a useful kitchen aid can also be an expressive and colourful object. The hand-modelled spoons are made to collect and display.

feet

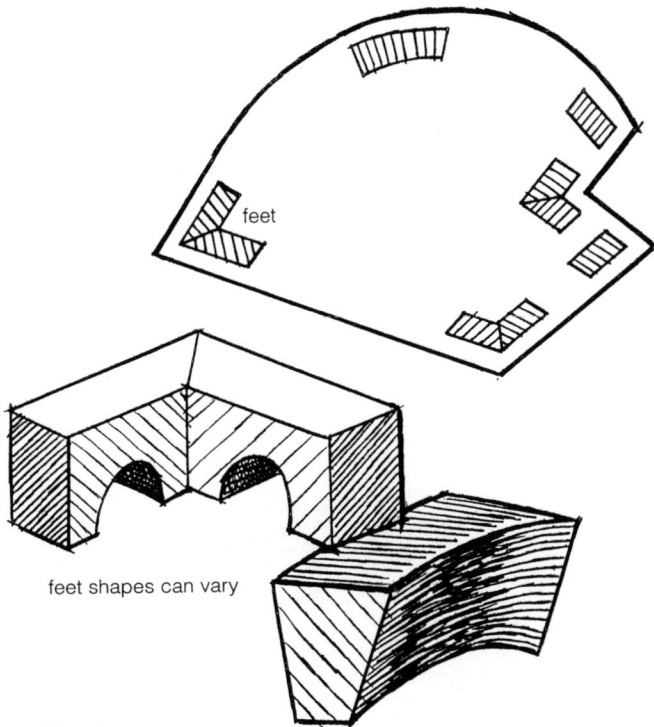

feet shapes can vary

12 Large Herb Planter

Ⓘ
Ⓐ

Using drape and coil techniques in combination, this project draws on the skills of joining, paddling, and forming large amounts of clay to build containers for use in the garden.

Materials

Earthenware terracotta clay or Feeneys BRT (stoneware)
Black copper oxide
Coloured slips.

To form

• Roll a large number of coils 20 mm thick and 600 mm long. Follow the instructions for *Coiling* on page 18.
• Following the instructions for *Clay Slabs* on page 17, roll out a slab of clay of 12–15 mm thick for the base. For a large planter this should be 40 cm in diameter; for a medium planter, 30 cm in diameter; for a small planter, 25 cm in diameter.
• Using a shallow-curved round puki, drape mould as instructed on page 20. This forms the base of the herb planter, which is slightly curved.
• Roughen the surface around the circumference of the circle and paint with slurry.
• Position and build up coils as described for the bowls (page 41).
• When you have reached the desired height (approximately 30 cm for large planters, 25 cm for medium or 20 cm for small), add the final rim coil. This needs to be slightly thicker than the coils for the walls of the planter. Paddle the pot all around and allow to set to leatherhard by drying slowly.

To decorate

• Lightly draw the pattern or design of your choice onto the outside walls and the rim.
• Apply shellac—by using a paintbrush, by sponging, or by spattering with a toothbrush, to achieve an interesting texture. Allow to dry. The shellac will act as a resist. Make certain the shellac is dry before beginning washback.
• Wash back with a damp sponge. The areas of clay that have not been painted with shellac will wash away, creating depressions in the clay. When the piece has been fired, the shellacked areas will appear raised, creating an overall effect of low-relief. Repeat any number of times to create the depth of pattern you require. Allow the piece to dry.
• Paint black or white slip into the washed areas to create the effect of inlay. Sponge lightly to remove excess slip from shellacked areas. Allow the planter to dry thoroughly, then load for firing.

When using this washback technique, or painting on slip, do not allow the dried piece to get too wet, or joins will pop apart (water causes clay to swell).

To fire

• Single-fire BRT clay in an electric kiln (oxidation) to 1240°C or in a gas kiln (reduction) to 1250°C.
• Single-fire red raku clay in an electric or a gas kiln to 1120°C.

Slow, even heating and complete cooling of the kiln before unloading will help prevent dunting or warping.

Lay slab into puki and cut a circle to match your required diameter

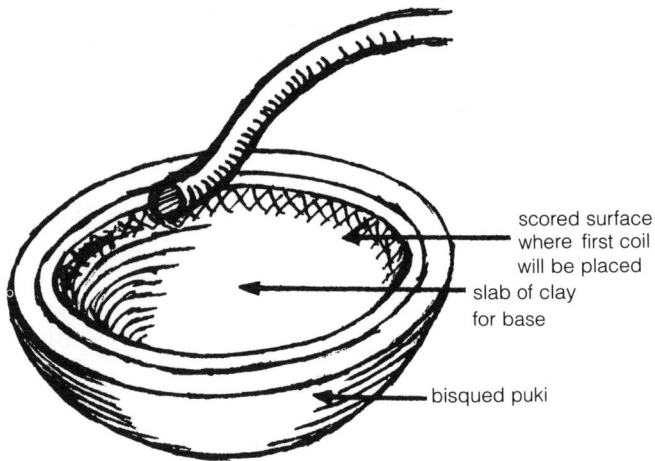

Adding coils to base

To finish

• Finish as described for the bowls (page 42).

To add drainage holes

• Gently turn the planter rim-down on a piece of foam or soft towelling and place a series of drainage holes in the bottom using a nail or clay knife.

Feet are used on this planter to raise it off the ground slightly, allowing for drainage. The feet must be sufficiently wide and sturdy to support the planter and be visually strong. Three feet are required, arranged in a triangle for stability.

To form and attach feet

• Form feet by rolling balls of clay (about 25 mm in diameter), slicing from cylinders of rolled clay, or cutting out of thick-cut slabs of clay.
• Attach feet as for spice containers (page 43).

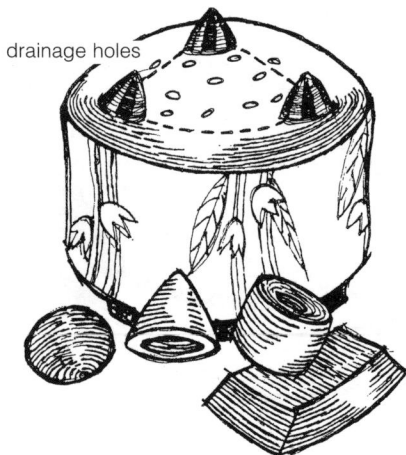

Different foot shapes; note triangular arrangement

To decorate

• You can use several methods to impress texture into the pot before it is leatherhard. A wooden paddle that has rope glued on it makes a good tool for paddling texture into a pot. Various items may be used to press into the clay. Lines may be scored, cross-hatched or carved into the surface. Shapes may be cut from slabs of clay and joined by the score/slurry method. Coils and small balls of clay may be paddled onto the surface. Lino which is used for lino-block printing may be carved, then glued onto wood paddles or made into stamps to press and paddle texture into the surface.
• Sgraffito lines through slip.

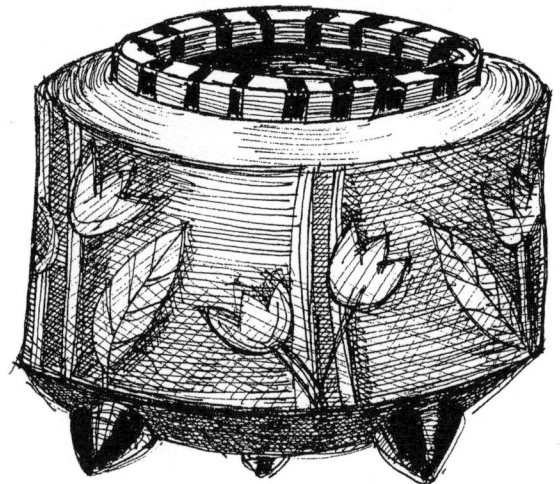

• Sgraffito lines or patterns into the leatherhard clay and fill with a mixture of copper oxide and water, using a paintbrush. Sponge back over the lines so that the copper stays in the lines—when fired the lines will appear black. Paint slip on the surface, being careful not to obscure the lines.
• Further enhance the texture or low relief that you have added to the surface by painting with copper wash, then sponging back over the high points. The copper will stay in the texture, creating contrast between the high and low areas of the relief.
• Paint layers of coloured slip onto the texture, then wipe back with a sponge, creating further contrast and colour. A light scouring with steel wool or a green plastic scourer will create a scumbled effect.

To fire

• Single-fire in a gas or an electric kiln. Earthenware terracotta should be fired to 1040–1100°C, and Feeneys BRT to 1100–1250°C.

Ⓒ *13 Birdbath*
Ⓘ
Ⓐ

This project combines draped slab, coil and modelling techniques to form separate parts which, once fired, are threaded onto a piece of iron rebar and glued together to create a birdbath/garden sculpture. Contrast of textured surfaces and cut-slab decoration are also explored in this project.

Materials

Earthenware clays such as Keenes Raku T, white earthenware (SWE from Clayworks), or terracotta (Delclay or Walkers)
A comb and other tools for texturing surface of clay
A large curved former such as a wok
20 mm iron rebar
2-part epoxy glue
Small metal rod.

You will need to decide at the outset how many components you wish to make and the final height you want your birdbath to be. A finished height of 90 cm is standard, but the iron rebar will need to be about 120 cm long so that you can push it into the ground for added stability. The birdbath pictured opposite page 17 has thirteen separate pieces.

To form

- Roll out the number of slabs you will require for the discs and bowl form. A thickness of 10–12 mm is ideal for the slab.

decorative discs

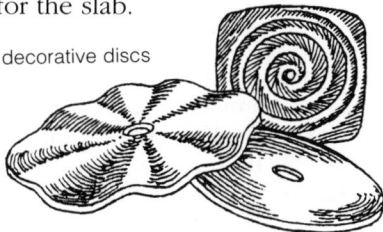

- Lay the slabs inside or on top of their formers and texture the exposed surfaces while they are supported. Pay attention to the edges of the discs—you may wish to pinch them, round or scallop them (see drawing). Allow to set up. Cut a 30 mm hole in the centre of all the discs to allow them to be threaded over the rebar once fired.
- For the bowl of the birdbath, which sits on top of the stand, roll a slab 40–50 cm in diameter or make two slabs and join them together thoroughly. To obtain a circular shape, attach a small nail to a string, hold the string in the centre of the slab and trace a line on the clay with the nail, holding the string tight and moving it around the centre point. This will give you an even circle.
- If you have draped inside a former, work on the inside and the rim of the bowl before removing it from the former. Strengthen the rim with an additional slab or coil of clay. Cut a 30 mm hole in the

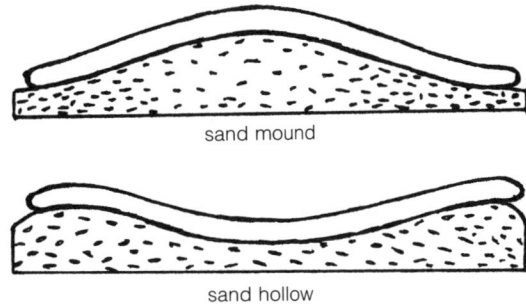

sand mound

sand hollow

centre of the bowl form to allow it to sit on top of the rebar (which will go up the centre inside the cone-centrepiece).

- Coil the cone centrepiece which will support the bird and join it onto the bowl in the centre while the bowl is at soft to leatherhard stage. It is best to support it in the former while this is done. Cut an opening 10 mm in diameter in the top of the cone so that the bird may be attached later.
- Texture the inside of the bowl, or apply cut slab shapes inside and/or on the rim. To join slab shapes, score and slip both surfaces.
- Incorporate a ledge or perches into the rim, to allow birds to perch while bathing.

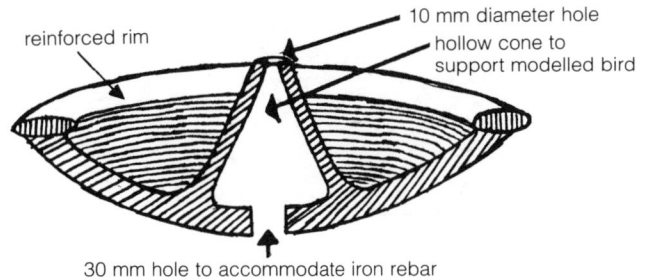

reinforced rim
10 mm diameter hole
hollow cone to support modelled bird
30 mm hole to accommodate iron rebar

- Model animals, birds, etc. for the rim and centrepiece and attach at making stage or glue on after firing. Draw the shape of your choice on newspaper and cut out to make a template. Roll a slab, lay the template on the slab and cut out. Repeat—you will need two sides.
- Lay one cut bird slab on your work surface, place small pieces of scrunched-up newspaper inside the head and body (these will burn out when fired), then lay the second bird-slab on top. Join

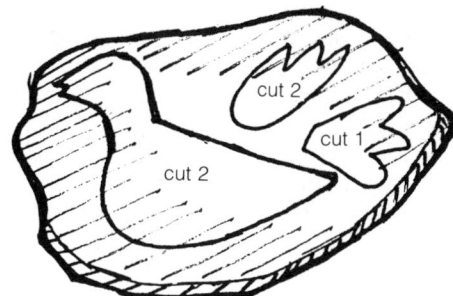

cut 2
cut 1
cut 2

51

all around the edges by pinching together, then smooth the joins over. Model the shape further using wooden modelling tools, adding wings, tail, beak and other features as you desire.

- Cut a hole in the bottom of the bird, or add a narrow cylinder of clay which will fit a small metal rod inside. The bird sits on the rod (like a lollipop) and then you glue the rod into the cone in the centre of the birdbath when all pieces have been fired and are ready to assemble.

Alternatively, you may wish to keep your bird as a flat slab shape, or make the forms by the coiling method. There are many different approaches to modelling.

- Using coils, form cone shapes for the birdbath stand. The base cone should have a diameter of approximately 300 mm at the bottom narrowing to 50 mm at the top.
- Dry all components slowly. Remember: large pieces require longer to dry.

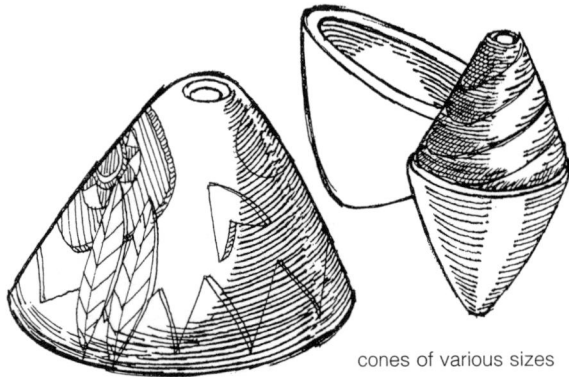

cones of various sizes

To decorate

Use a combination of the techniques listed below.

- Impressed texture—At the making stage, when the clay is still soft, textures may be impressed into the clay by stamping, paddling or rolling.
- Sgraffito lines into the surface when pieces are stiffening.
- Carving at leatherhard stage with metal clay tools or old dental tools.
- Slip trailing—This may be done using slip made of the same clay as that used for the birdbath, or the white slip recipe given on page 60. The slip needs to be stiffer than that used for painting, to give a raised line. Slip trailing works best from the leatherhard stage up to dry stage, providing the slip is compatible with the clay body.
- Painted clay surfaces—For adding texture to a clay surface, dribble a thick slurry of the clay used for the birdbath over your piece. Comb or work into the slip with various tools, then allow it to set up. The additional moisture in the slip will soften the piece you are painting on, so the leatherhard to

dry stage would be the best time to do this, to avoid collapsing the piece. Dry work slowly before adding copper wash or coloured slips.

- Copper and/or manganese washes—Copper or manganese mixed with water and painted on the dried pieces, then washed back with a sponge, will further highlight the texture of the surfaces by leaving black in the depressions. The copper or manganese will tend to bleed through additional layers of coloured slips, giving an antique-like effect. Combined with the technique of scumbling of coloured slips, some very interesting effects can be obtained.
- Slip washes—On top of the manganese or copper, layers of coloured slip of varying consistencies may be painted, then scrubbed back using a green kitchen scourer or fine steel wool. In this way, a multi-coloured antique-like surface is built up. Additional layers of copper and slip will increase the appearance of depth.
- Scumbling—White or coloured slips of a thick, dry consistency are scumbled onto the surface using bristle brushes. In combination with the above techniques, rich textural effects may be achieved. A fresh approach and a desire to experiment will enable original effects to be achieved.

To bisque

- Once dried, bisque-fire all decorated pieces in kiln to 1000°C.

To glaze

- Glaze the inside of the bird bath bowl up to the edge where the rim begins, and the centre cone. Use turquoise clear glaze Δ05–03 on light or white clay, or peacock blue Δ05–03 on all clays, including terracotta (see recipes, page 61).

To load and fire

- Load all pieces, with the exception of the inside bowl of the bird bath, fairly close together as oxides and slips will not stick. Avoid packing pieces inside one another as manganese and copper washes will tend to flux the slips together.
- Fire in oxidation in an electric kiln to 1060–1120°C.

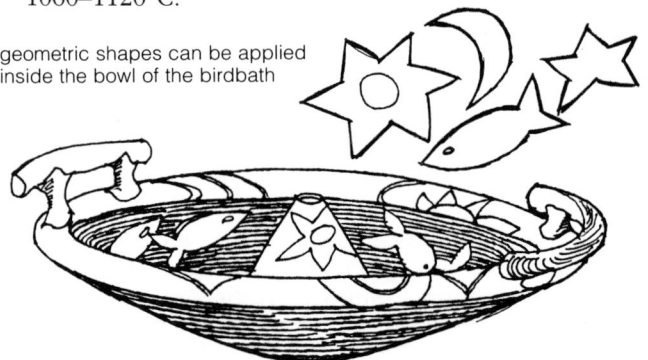

geometric shapes can be applied inside the bowl of the birdbath

(I)
(A)

14   *Pedestal Planter*

In this project basic slab construction is explored using simple two-dimensional cardboard templates as cutting guides for the clay slabs. The end result is a distinctive plant container to be used as a centre-piece for a garden table.

Materials

Any earthenware clay, such as terracotta (I used white earthenware) providing it is fairly porous (a stoneware clay that has an open texture could also be used, providing a drain hole is placed in the bottom of the plant container)
Carved lino stamps
Sieve for straining slip
Slip trailer.

Lino (the type used for lino-block printing) that has had texture or pattern carved into the surface makes ideal stamps for creating low-relief patterns or images on the clay's surface, simply by pressing or rolling the carved lino into a slab of rolled clay. Lino can be used for small stamped patterns that repeat, tiles, and larger clay slabs which are then cut using templates and assembled into a variety of objects such as the planter in this project.

To carve the lino

- So that you can see the patterns you are carving into the lino, it is helpful to coat the lino first with india ink. Soften lino by warming in a low oven (leave door open). Lino is much easier to carve when soft.
- When using lino-carving tools, always hold the lino with one hand and carve *away* from that hand, so as not to incur injury.
- Dust the lino with powdered clay or talc to allow the lino to release easily from the clay slab without sticking.
- Small lino stamps will require a wooden block backing. Use PVA to glue stamp to wood. This will provide a handle for stamping.

To design the planter

The pedestal planter consists of three parts: the container, which holds the plant; the decorative rim, which prevents earth and water from spilling out; and the raised pedestal upon which the planter sits.

The pedestal is made and fired separately from the planter in order that the planter may be easily moved for planting and watering. The pedestal serves to raise the planter from the table and adds decorative interest. It is important that the planter and its pedestal be compatible in style.

You may vary the style of your planter from the one shown here providing you draw your ideas first and then translate them into templates.

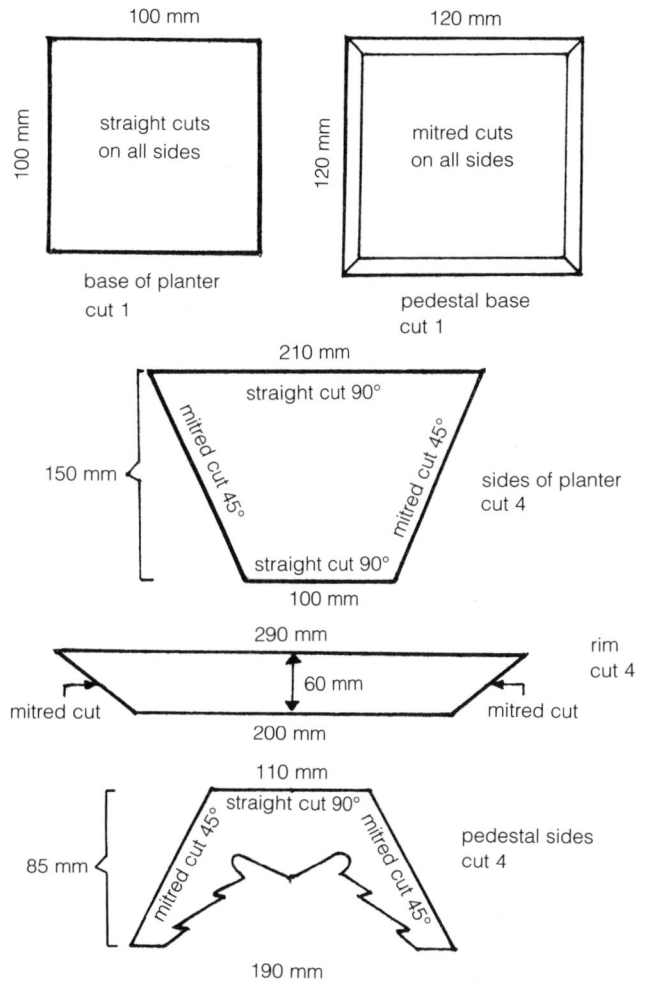

100 mm × 100 mm — straight cuts on all sides — base of planter cut 1

120 mm × 120 mm — mitred cuts on all sides — pedestal base cut 1

210 mm, straight cut 90°, mitred cut 45°, 150 mm, mitred cut 45°, straight cut 90°, 100 mm — sides of planter cut 4

290 mm, 60 mm, mitred cut, mitred cut, 200 mm — rim cut 4

110 mm, mitred cut 45°, straight cut 90°, mitred cut 45°, 85 mm, mitred cut 45°, mitred cut 45°, 190 mm — pedestal sides cut 4

To make the templates

- Using a pencil and a metal ruler, draw the pattern pieces onto cardboard, following the dimensions below. If you want the planter smaller or larger, adjust accordingly by scaling up or down. (A photocopier that enlarges and reduces will do this easily.)

Note: It is useful to make cardboard templates and assemble with masking tape to check that they fit together properly before cutting into clay slabs.

To roll clay slabs

- Roll out slabs to a thickness of approximately 10 mm (see *Clay Slabs*, page 17). Ensure all slabs are the same thickness.

To texture slabs with lino stamps

- While the slabs of clay are still soft, use your lino stamps and texture squares to impress into the clay. If you are impressing with a large piece of lino, lay it on top of the clay slab and roll it gently with a rolling pin to obtain an even impression. Peel the lino back carefully from the corner.

- Once you are satisfied with the amount of pattern or texture on your slabs, allow them to stiffen, ready for cutting.

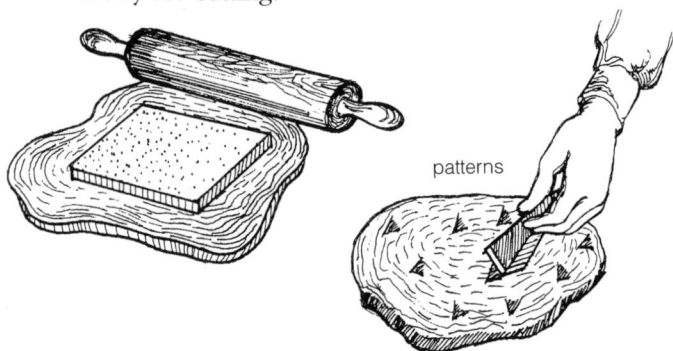

Roll larger pieces of textured lino with a rolling pin

To cut slabs

- Using templates (see page 17), cut out the required shapes. Ensure that you cut on a 45° angle where indicated (see template for angles), to create the mitred joint. Bases are cut straight (at 90°) unless otherwise stated on templates.

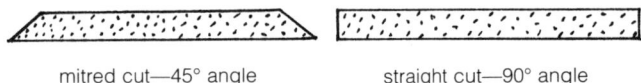

mitred cut—45° angle   straight cut—90° angle

- Remove cut pieces to a cement board to stiffen up, with templates still on top to minimise distortion.

To assemble

- When the slabs are stiff enough to stand without bending (just before leatherhard stage), assemble as for the bonsai planter (page 47), in the following order: Start with the base. Add wall A to base. Add wall B to base and side A. Add wall C to base and side B. Add wall D to base and sides C and A. Add rim (which has been assembled as above) on top of A–B–C–D.

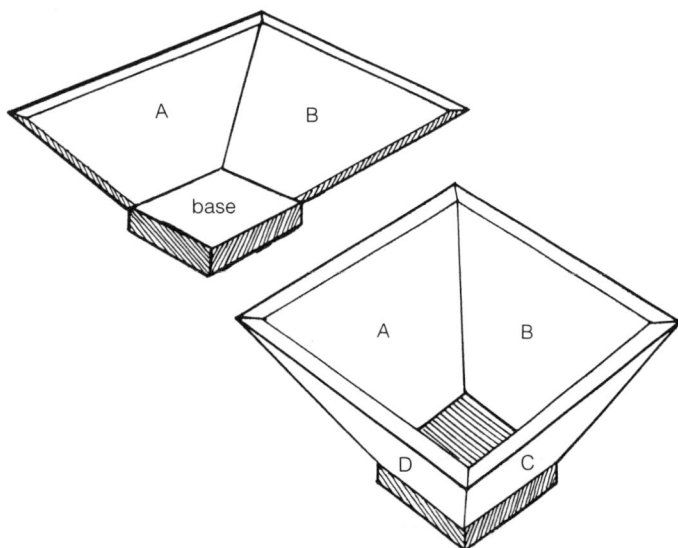

To form the pedestal

- Form the pedestal upside-down by repeating the procedure for the planter.

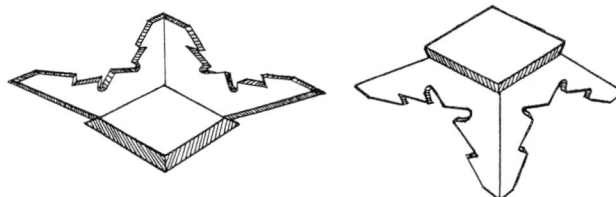

To dry and clean up

- Wrap pieces in plastic to equalise moisture and allow even drying. When both planter and base are firm, check that the planter fits the pedestal, and that both pieces sit flat. Complete final clean-up and detailing at this stage.

If your planter is made of stoneware clay which will be fired higher than earthenware clay, cut a drainage hole in the base at this stage.

To decorate

- Before pieces are dry, you can use slip trailing (see page 21) to add further visual interest and link the texture created by the lino-stamping. The white slip made using the recipe on page 60 is ideal for trailing. This needs to be of stiffer consistency than when used for painting, in order that the lines you trail will be raised. Sieve through a 100-mesh sieve to remove lumps.
- Once all the slip-trailing you wish to do has been completed, allow the slip to stiffen-up, then cover the pedestal planter and dry slowly.
- When dry, you can enhance the textured surfaces of the planter.
  Paint washes of copper and/or manganese onto the piece then sponge back, leaving oxide in the texture and giving contrast to the low relief.
  Then paint on layers of coloured slips and sponge or rub back, providing colour and depth to the surface. By dry-scumbling slip onto slip, laying oxide washes on, then layers of painted slip, you can achieve many rich or subtle variations to the surface.
- Allow the piece to dry completely.

To load and fire

- Single-fire earthenware clays in an electric kiln to 1060°C.
- Single-fire stoneware clays in either an electric or gas kiln to 1240–1280°C.

After firing, you may wish to give some protection to the slip-decorated surface by waxing lightly with beeswax. This is easily done by warming the planter up in a slow oven, then painting the beeswax on and rubbing back with a soft cloth. The surface of your piece will have a slight sheen.

(C)
(I)
(A)

15 Hanging Birdhouse

Basic slab construction from cardboard templates is used in this project in conjunction with modelled additions to create a unique, usable hanging birdhouse for the garden.

Materials

Any fine earthenware terracotta clay
Wooden dowel and rope.

The birdhouse consists of four sections: the base, walls, roof and ridgepole. The proportions of the birdhouse will depend on the type of bird you wish to house. The hole or door needs to be wide enough to accommodate its intended occupant, but not so wide that it will allow rain to enter. A diameter of 40–45 mm would be suitable for a medium-sized bird such as a rosella. The hole must be located three-quarters of the way up the chamber, towards the top. This will allow adequate nesting space below.

It is wise for the roof to overhang, or have eaves front and back, as further protection from weather and rain run-off. Some birds will require a perch in front of the entry hole; perches around the base of the birdhouse will allow landing space.

To make the templates

• Using a pencil and metal ruler, draw the pattern pieces onto cardboard. If you wish to vary the design or size of the birdhouse from the one suggested, simply alter the templates.

Note: It is useful to assemble the cardboard templates with masking tape to check that they fit together properly before cutting into clay slabs.

To roll and cut slabs, and assemble

• Roll out slabs to a thickness of 10 mm (see *Clay Slabs*, page 17).
• Assemble as for the pedestal planter.
• Place the base slab on a kiln shelf that has been dusted lightly with grog.
• Cut an entry hole from the front (A) and place the front in position on the base, allowing approximately 50 mm each side, 30 mm in front (see illustration).
• Attach side C to base and front, side D to front (A), and back (B) to sides C and D, using the method described on page 48.
• Roughen the inside surfaces of the birdhouse to allow baby birds to grip and climb around.
• Slot the ridgepole into place—along the top of the peak, and jutting out at the front, back and top. Secure inside and outside with coils and smooth

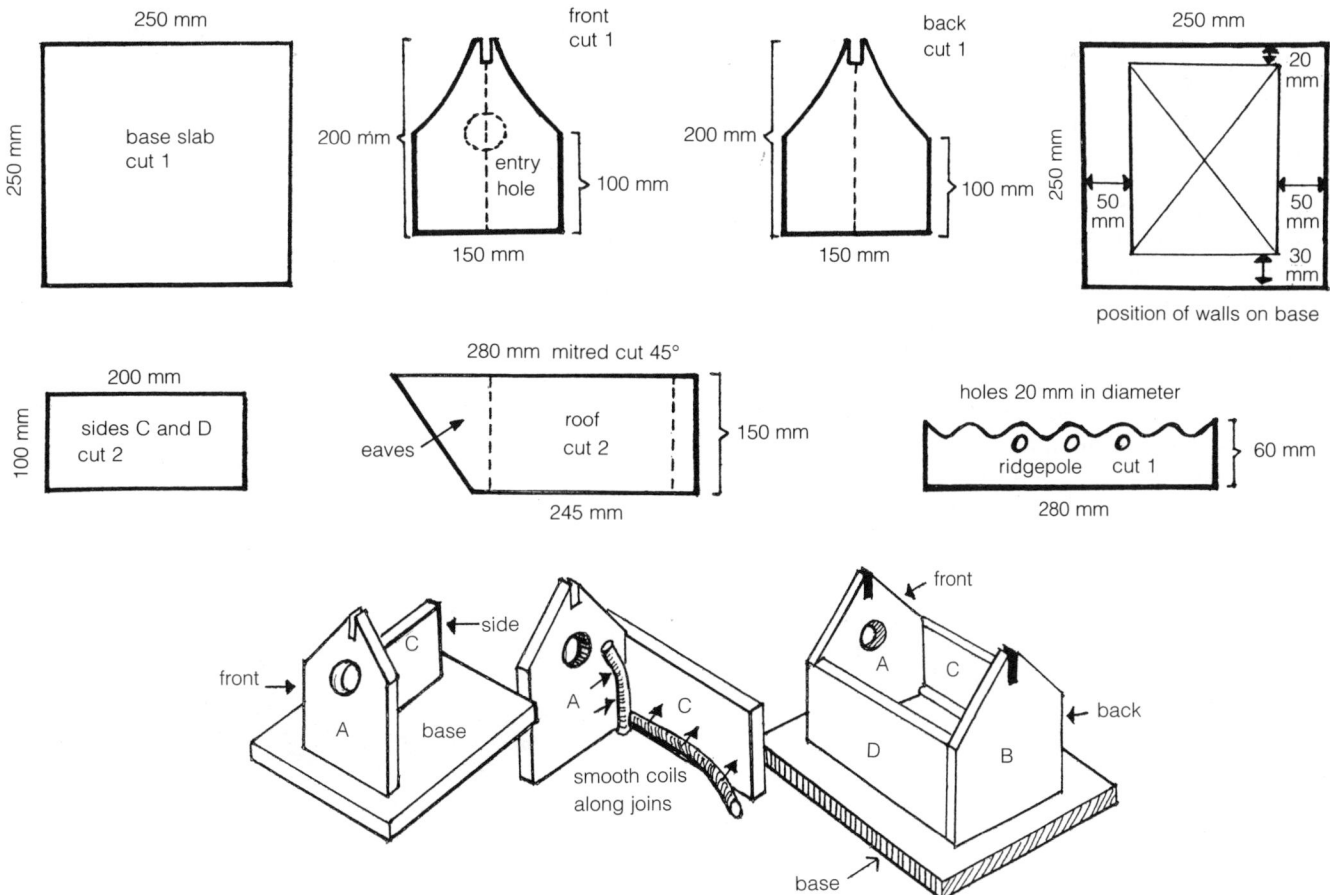

base slab cut 1 — 250 mm × 250 mm

front cut 1 — 200 mm, 150 mm, 100 mm, entry hole

back cut 1 — 200 mm, 150 mm, 100 mm

250 mm, 20 mm, 50 mm, 50 mm, 30 mm, 250 mm — position of walls on base

sides C and D cut 2 — 200 mm × 100 mm

280 mm mitred cut 45° — roof cut 2, eaves, 150 mm, 245 mm

holes 20 mm in diameter — ridgepole cut 1, 60 mm, 280 mm

front, side, C, A, base

smooth coils along joins, A, C, base

front, A, C, D, B, back, base

into place. The holes in the ridgepole must sit above the roofline as they will hold the wooden dowel for hanging the birdhouse.

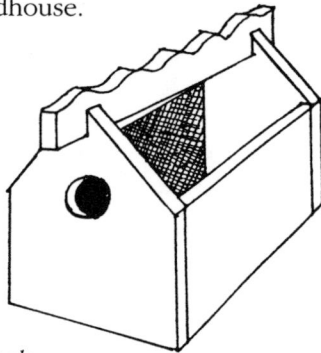

Placing the ridgepole

- Mitre the top of the roof where it will join the ridgepole, and lay it in place to follow the slight curve on the front and back walls. It will extend on either side and front and back to create eaves.

To decorate

- Model additions to the ridgepole, eaves and front and attach. (I have modelled a bird's head and tail to either end of the ridgepole, added decorative braces under the eaves using flattened coils, and built a small perch in front of the entry hole.)
- Add other decorative features to the walls and around the edge of the base. (I have made perches around the front and sides of the base, and modelled features around the hole where the wooden dowel will go through for hanging the birdhouse, and the entry hole.)
- Sgraffito further detail onto the birdhouse using a bamboo skewer.
- Wrap the piece in plastic and allow to dry *slowly* on the kiln shelf.
- Once the birdhouse has completely dried (this may take up to one week, with extended periods of unwrapping and ventilating), paint copper wash into sgraffitoed lines, then sponge back to enhance details.
- Paint with slip—perhaps using white only, painting it over the terracotta in areas, then washing back to give an antique effect; or using coloured slips. Your own decorations will give your birdhouse character and originality. You could also use many of the techniques of decorating with slip from previous projects if you wish to further extend this project.
- Remember not to saturate the birdhouse with wet oxide or slip—it will spring apart! Paint small areas of slip at one time, then allow them to dry.

To dry, load and fire

- Allow the birdhouse to dry thoroughly again.
- Load, and single-fire slowly in an electric or gas kiln to 1060°C.

16 Wall Planter

Ⓢ Ⓑ Ⓘ Ⓐ

Designed to be wall-mounted in a garden, this planter is ideal for a variety of flowers, plants or even fruit such as strawberries. It combines slab and draped slab techniques with modelling, and glaze and slip decoration.

Materials

Fine earthenware terracotta clay
4 x 50 mm rustproof counter-sinking screws
Silicon sealer for screwholes.

The size of your wall planter will be determined by the type of plant you wish to grow in it, and where you want to mount it.

A cardboard template may be made for the back if you wish.

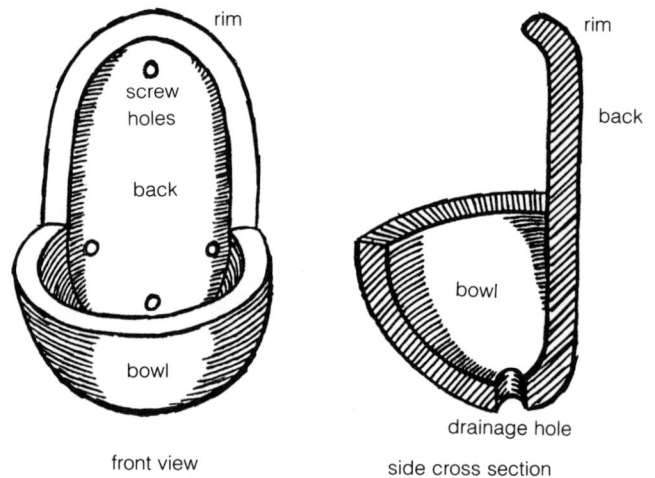

front view   side cross section

To form the back slab

- Roll slabs, as described on page 17, to a thickness of 10 mm and the size you require. If using the template, lay it on the slab and cut around the edges.
- Transfer the cut slab to cement sheeting. Place cotton wadding, foam, or a large coil of clay under the outside edge of the back slab all the way around to give the edge a gentle curve upwards. (You will need to separate the clay coil from the clay slab with sheets of newspaper.) This will support the curved edge until it has set up.
- Allow to set up.

cotton wadding support
helps to curve rim

Support outside edge of slab with a clay coil or cotton wadding to curve it all around

To form the bowl

- Drape the slab over a bisque or plaster bowl former and leave to set up.
- With a sharp clay knife cut the bowl either in half or two-thirds to create the form which will be the container for the soil and plant.

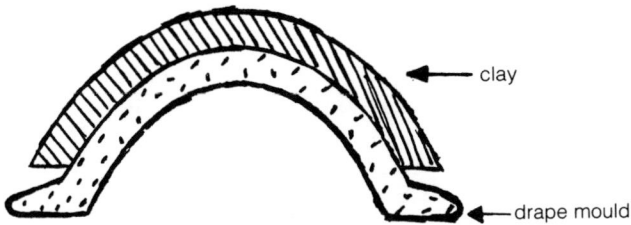

To join bowl to back

- Score and slip the cut edge of the bowl, and the back slab where the bowl will be joined. Place bowl on the slab and push firmly into position. Place a coil along the inside join of the bowl and smooth into place. Join outside of bowl to slab back by smoothing the join, then trim excess back slab away.
- Allow to stiffen.

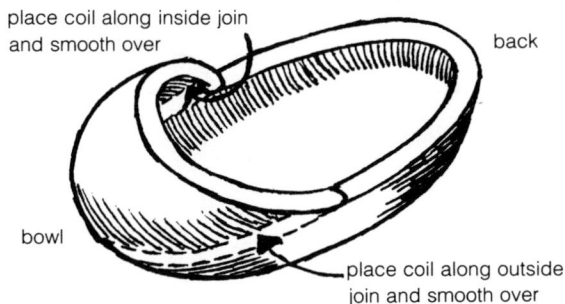

To place holes

Mark position for drainage holes in the bottom of the bowl, then drill with a large nail or turn the point of a clay knife until it is through to the other side. (Holes should be about 15 mm in diameter.) Similarly cut four screw holes, approximately 10 mm diameter (clay will shrink in drying and firing), in the back of the planter. Clean excess clay from holes.

To add the rim

Finish the edge of the bowl and back of the planter with a rounded rim of clay about 20–25 mm wide and 10 mm thick, cut from a flat slab of clay or flattened to the required size from a fat coil. Once you

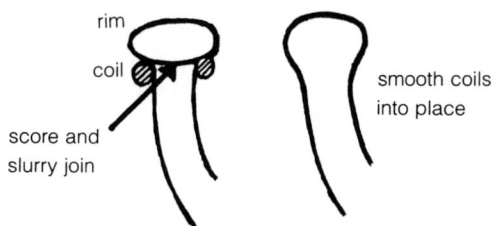

have placed the rim along all of the back edge, repeat for the bowl section.

To decorate

- Model a variety of small creatures, plants, insects, fish, in fact any subject matter that will relate to the garden theme and attach to the wall planter with slip. Remember to make the modelled pieces no thicker than 25 mm of solid clay. (I modelled a small cat sleeping on the rim of this planter.)
- Sgraffito patterns or motifs into the clay using a bamboo skewer. (I sgraffitoed plant and flower forms into the clay's surface.)
- Allow the wall planter to dry slowly on a cement board or kiln shelf with grog sprinkled between the board and clay—this will enable the slab to contract easily as it dries.
- Coat the inside of the planter bowl and back, which is going to be glazed, with white slip painted or poured on. The glaze will appear brighter on this white surface.
- Lay in oxide as described on page 50, and allow to dry thoroughly before attempting any further decoration.
- Coloured slip can be painted on inside or around the sgraffitoed lines for additional colour and interest.
- Once decoration is complete, dry thoroughly.

To bisque

- Bisque-fire to 1000°C in kiln.

To glaze

- Using the turquoise or peacock blue (see recipes, page 61) pour or paint glaze inside the planter.
- Temporarily block the screw holes and drainage holes with soft clay if you are pouring glaze inside the bowl. Clean the holes with a small clay knife once glaze is dry.
- Do not glaze the outside of the planter.

To load and fire

- Clean any excess glaze from the outside of the planter. Sprinkle a kiln shelf with grog or alumina hydrate to prevent cracking during shrinkage.
- Load and fire in an electric or a gas kiln (oxidation) to 1060°C.

To assemble

- Screw four screws 40–50 mm long through the holes, into a wall or post behind. Seal the screw holes with silicon sealant to prevent any leakage when watering. If mounting to masonry, use cement screws. If you want a permanent mounting, use screws and bondcrete.
- Place gravel inside your planter before adding a good potting mix.

Ⓒ
Ⓑ
Ⓘ
Ⓐ

17 Hanging Garden Screen

This project focuses on the exploration of form, elements and principles of design such as repetition, contrast, balance, composition, size and scale. The end result is a hanging screen which adds interest to any garden setting and complements the greenery.

Materials

Fine earthenware terracotta
Galvanised nails and U-nails
5 mm diameter strong twisted wire, rustproof.

Designing your screen

This screen is made up of a variety of three-dimensional forms. To create these forms, start by playing with the clay: pinching, rolling, twisting and cutting (see *Basic Forming Techniques*, pages 16–20). Experiment to see what kind of forms you can create. It is ideal to make lots of forms of the same shape, varying their size or proportions slightly. This will lend unity to the screen when assembled.

The number of forms you will need depends on the size of the screen you wish to make, and the size of your forms. It is probably easier to determine the size of the screen's frame first, then make lots of pieces which you feel will work together. Decorate and fire the forms before working out your final sizing and assembly.

There are a number of considerations in this exercise:

• Use a variety of forms that will work together.
• All forms must have a hole through them so that they may be strung onto the wire.
• Forms must not be too thick—solid clay more than 2.5 cm thick tends to blow up in the kiln, or is too heavy.

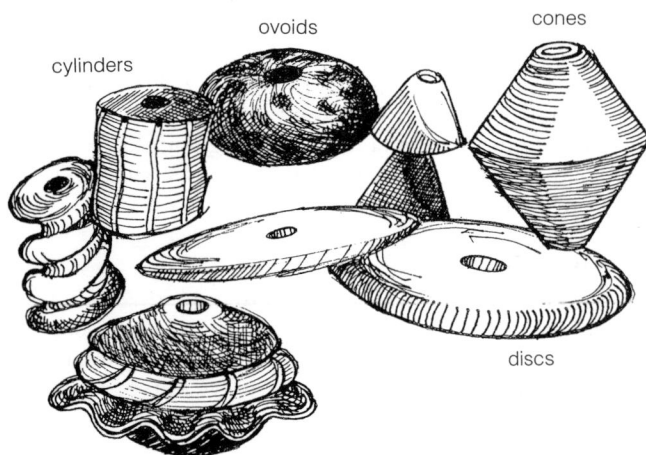

cylinders
ovoids
cones
discs

A variety of forms

• Forms must not be too wide (they will interfere with the forms hung beside them), or too delicate (they will break in the wind).

Treat the forms as though they were giant beads. Use smaller, simpler forms (such as balls of clay and cylinders) as spacers between the larger, more intricate ones, unifying the complete screen.

You can texture the forms by rolling them on textured surfaces or over pieces of string or rope taped to a flat surface. A ruler rolled over the clay on its edge will make ridges or divisions indented into the form.

To make holes

• Make holes through the centre of the forms while they are still soft. Insert a nail or a large bamboo skewer through the form until it can be seen poking out the other side. Instead of continuing to push the skewer straight through, pull it back out and push it into the side it was coming through. This avoids a burred edge of clay on the exit side.

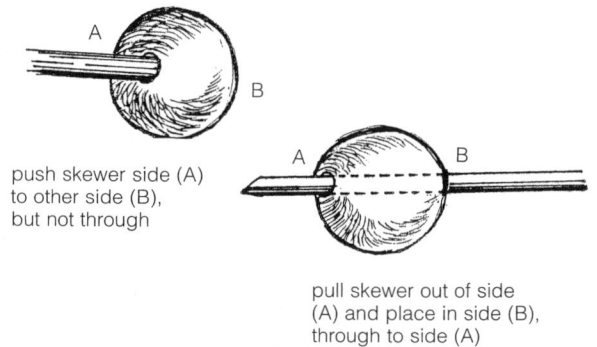

push skewer side (A) to other side (B), but not through

pull skewer out of side (A) and place in side (B), through to side (A)

• Roll the form as for the candlestick to enlarge the hole. (You might like to roll the form onto a textured surface while the skewer is inside the hole performing two functions at once.)
• When you remove the skewer, press both ends of the hole with your thumb and forefinger to flatten any rough edges around the hole.
• Dry the form to leatherhard stage, then clean the hole further if necessary using a small clay knife. Sgraffito linear decoration into the surface at this stage. Alternatively, you may wish to paint coloured slips on the forms and sgraffito through the slip at a slightly drier stage.

To decorate

If you have sgraffitoed into some of your shapes at leatherhard stage, or textured them while soft, you can paint them once dry with copper wash and sponge back to emphasise the lines you have made. You may then wish to paint with coloured slip. It is wise to limit the colours to two or three slips, and not paint all the forms, allowing the red terracotta clay to predominate. If you use too much colour and pattern, the screen will look too busy and not unified. Sgraffito may be done through the coloured slip to the red clay body underneath, giving red lines. Keep painted slip patterns bold and simple; forms will be varied and the colour is added as accent mainly.

To fire

- Single-fire the forms slowly to 1060°C in an oxidising atmosphere. Pieces may be carefully stacked on top of or against one another as they are not glazed so will not stick together.

To prepare the frame

- Construct the frame from treated pine, which should be stained or painted before you assemble it. Wooden posts 10–11 cm x 3 cm will provide adequate support for the size of screen illustrated.
- Measure the wood, cut and construct the frame, and drill the holes that the wire will go through before threading forms onto wire and placing them in the frame.

To compose and assemble the shapes

- Lay all your forms on a large, flat surface and arrange (without threading onto wire) in a line of the required length. Make adjustments to the arrangement of the forms at this stage before threading them onto the wire. If you work on one length at a time, then thread the arrangement onto the wire, you will be able to move the lengths around to ascertain which ones look best together before placing them in the screen.

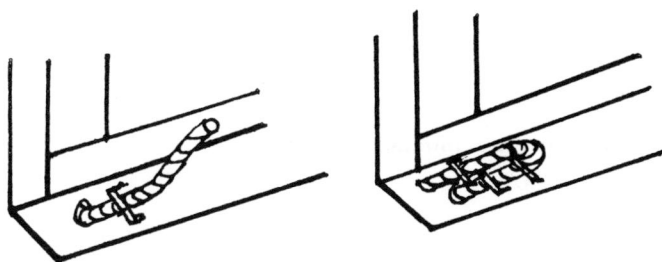

secure wire to frame with U-nails

- For the size of screen illustrated, approximately 12 lengths of wire of 2.5 metres will be required.

To thread shapes onto wire

- Once you have the linear arrangement of forms ready, thread onto wire. Ensure that the forms are evenly balanced and weighted. Leave both ends of wire free in case you need to add or take away forms when hanging the screen.

To hang the forms on the frame

- You will need two people to hang the lengths of forms onto the frame.
- Lay the lengths of forms down, one at a time, in front of the frame. Have one person hold the top of the length while the other threads the bottom through the first hole at the bottom of the frame. Anchor the wire underneath by hammering a U-shaped nail over the wire. Bend the wire back and hammer another U-shape nail over the top.
- The person holding the top of the length of forms now threads the wire through the top hole (underside) to the topside of the top frame. The wire will be very heavy and may sag. Pull as taut as possible. At this point you may need to remove or add small forms to get the length to fit the frame exactly. Once you have done this, hammer the wire in place (as before) with U-shaped nails. Repeat this procedure until all the lengths of form are in place.
- After a week, the wire may have stretched and sagged a little from the weight of the clay forms. To correct this, pull the wire at the top with pliers and re-anchor with U-nails. Excess wire may now be trimmed if necessary.

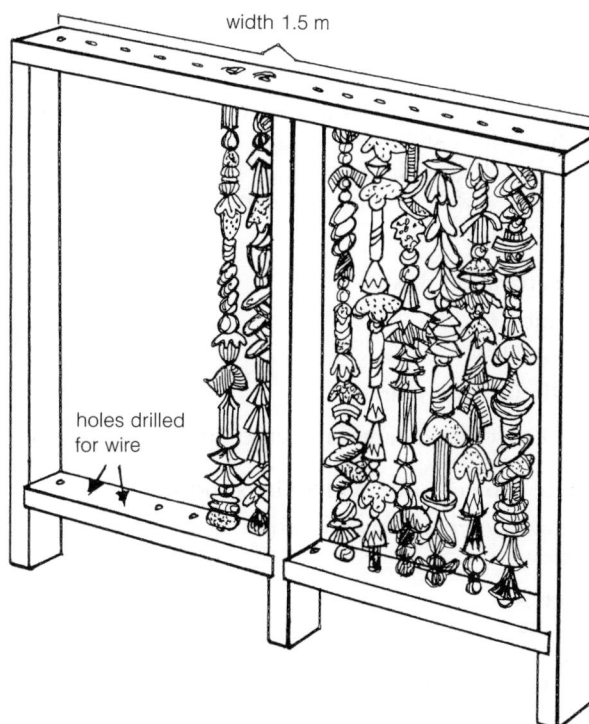

width 1.5 m

holes drilled for wire

Technical Information

Recipes

Kiln wash

Alumina hydrate	50%
Kaolin	50%

- Thin with water. Paint thickly on tops of shelves, one layer at a time.
- Sand back to produce a flat surface.
- Paint a thin coat on shelves.

Wadding mix

Fireclay	50%
Alumina hydrate	50%

- Mix into a soft clay consistency and roll into small wads or balls for use in stacking pots in a glaze firing.

Lid separation mix 1

$1/3$ flint (silica)
$2/3$ arrowroot

- Mix with water.
- Paint on unglazed surfaces such as lids, to prevent them from sticking.
- Keep off the glazed parts.
- Water and a toothbrush remove dry flint residue after firing.

Lid separation mix 2

Alumina hydrate
Hot paraffin

- Mix in equal parts.

These two lid separation recipes are interchangeable.

White slip coloured with oxides and stains

Suitable for earthenware white or terracotta clay and stoneware clay.

Batch A

Ball clay C	100 g	
Bentonite	5 g	Mix with 150 ml water
Frit 3110 or 4508	5 g	

Batch B
- Add an equal volume of white stoneware slip, porcelain slip or a slip made from your clay body (providing it is white or light in colour).
- To make the slip, dry clay and grind into a fine powder. 100 g of dry powder to 150 ml water will give a good consistency.

- Screen to remove lumps. Mix A and B together for a good slip base to add various colourants to.

Black slip

To the basic white slip recipe, add 2 tablespoons of black stain to 100 ml of wet slip, or, per 100 ml of wet slip add:

Black iron oxide	5 g
Manganese oxide	5 g
Cobalt oxide	5 g

Sieve through an 80-mesh screen and mix thoroughly with a paintbrush.

Brushwork blue pigment

To make a blue pigment for brushing under a clear glaze or on top of a raw white glaze, use a blue (underglaze or glaze) stain, mixed with medium to brushing consistency, and add this to a small amount of the glaze used on your piece.

Alternatively, you may wish to make a up a brushwork blue from the following ingredients:

Cobalt carbonate	20
Tin oxide	20
Kaolin	20
Terracotta clay	15
Manganese oxide	10
Talc	10
Iron oxide	5

Mix with water to an ink-like consistency.

Glazes

Earthenware clear gloss

1060–1260°C	Δ04–8
Frit 4113	85
Ball clay	15

Earthenware white gloss

1060–1260°C	Δ04–8
Frit 4113	85
Ball clay	15
Add: zircon	5
or tin	5

Zircon white

For use on terracotta clays

1100–1160°C	Δ03–2
Zircon frit 3302	79.66
Kaolin	12.23
Silica	8.09

Takes decoration well using stains or oxides and brush.

Semi-opaque glaze for terracotta clay

For use over clay slips

1160–1200°C	Δ3–5
Frit 3134	50
Potash feldspar	20
Ball clay	20
Magnesium carbonate	10
Add: tin oxide	10

Turquoise clear glaze Δ 05–03 for use on light or white clay bodies

Frit KMP 4110	80
Nepheline syenite	20
Copper carbonate	5

Peacock blue Δ 05–03 for use over all clays including terracotta

Frit KMP 4110	90
Kaolin	5
Lithium carbonate	5
Tin oxide	4
Copper carbonate	6

Suppliers and Ceramics Groups

Materials and Equipment

VICTORIA
Artisan Craft Books
Meat Market Centre,
42 Courtney Street, Nth Melbourne, 3051

B & L Tetlow Pty Ltd
12 George Street, Blackburn, 3130.
Phone (03) 9877 4188

Clayworks Australia Pty Ltd
6 Johnston Court, Dandenong, 3175.
Phone (03) 9791 6749
Suppliers of clear glazes—
#CEG-01-earthenware clear
#CMG-100-midfire clear

Northcote Pottery
85A Clyde Street, Thornbury, 3071.
Phone (03) 9484 4580

Port-O-Kiln Pty Ltd
63 Dandenong Street, Dandenong, 3175.
Phone (03) 9791 6799

Potters Equipment Pty Ltd
13/42 New Street, Ringwood, 3134.
Phone (03) 9870 7533

Walker Ceramics (Melbourne)
55 Lusher Road, Croydon, 3136.
Phone (03) 9725 7255

NEW SOUTH WALES
Keane Ceramics Pty Ltd
3971 Debenham Road, Somersby, 2250
Phone (04) 40 1069

Hilldav Electric Kilns and Potters' Warehouse
108 Oakes Road, Old Toongabbie, 2146
Phone (02) 688 1777

Hot and Sticky Pty Ltd
Steve Harrison Kilns and Clay Technology
Old School Railway Parade
Balmoral Village via Picton, 2571

The Puggoon Kaolin Company and Ceramic Supplies
PO Box 89, Gulgong, 2852
(clay and raw materials)

Walker Ceramics (Sydney)
51 Arthur Street, Forestville, 2087.
Phone (02) 451 5855

AUSTRALIAN CAPITAL TERRITORY
Walker Ceramics
289 Canberra Avenue, Fyshwick, 2609
Phone: (06) 280 5700

QUEENSLAND
Claycraft Supplies Pty Ltd
PO Box 1278, Fortitude Valley, 4006
Phone (07) 854 1515
(materials and equipment)

WESTERN AUSTRALIA
Venco Products
29 Owen Road, Kelmscot, WA 6111
Phone: (09) 399 5265
(pottery wheels and pug wheels)

Australian Ceramics Groups

The Victorian Ceramic Group Inc.
7 Blackwood Street, North Melbourne 3051.
Phone (03) 9329 1919
Bi-monthly newsletter.

The Potters' Society of Australia
68 Alexander Street, Crows Nest, NSW 2065.

The Potters' Guild of South Australia
P.O. Box 234, Stepney, SA 5069.

Glossary

Black core: The term applied to clay that has been fired too rapidly, without proper oxidation, from approximately 750° to 1000°C. This traps carbon inside the cross-section producing a black core, weakening the clay body and causing bloating at higher temperatures, and pin-holing in glazes.

Bone dry: The stage at which all the uncombined water in the clay has evaporated, and the clay is fully dry. This occurs during the bisque firing up to 400°C.

Cones: Pyrometric cones are made from mixtures of ceramic materials compressed into triangular cone shapes. They are designed to melt at given temperatures, and they provide a more accurate indication of the cumulative effect of heat inside the kiln than a simple temperature reading provides. The symbol for cone, Δ, is often used in glaze recipes to indicate the maturing temperature of a glaze.

Cottle: The walls that surround a form being cast in plaster. Made of lino, clay, cardboard or wood, this needs to be strong enough to contain the wet plaster until it has dried, when the cottle is easily removed.

Dunting: The cracking of ware in the kiln during the cooling process. This is caused by draughts of cool air entering the kiln and striking one part of the ware, causing it to contract more than the rest.

Earthenware: Pottery ware which remains porous and is fired from 800°C up to approximately 1150°C. Earthenware clays are generally red, brown or buff, although white earthenware is available. Earthenware may be glazed or unglazed.

Firing: Subjecting clay to temperatures which chemically change it.

Firing range: The range of temperatures within which clays can be effectively fired. The lowest point is 600°C, where the clay becomes *ceramic* and can no longer slake down in water. The highest is the clay's *vitrification* point, which can be as high as 1400°C for porcelain, but is usually around 1300°C for stoneware clay and up to 1150°C for earthenware.

Flux: Any ceramic material that lowers the melting point of a clay, glaze or colour. Glazes are often named after the main flux used in the glaze recipe, e.g. tin, magnesium, borax, etc.

Formers: Shapes made from craftwood, plaster, styrofoam or bisqued clay. Clay slabs are draped on top of positive formers or laid inside negative formers to create moulded pots.

Frit: Frits are made by heating, shattering and grinding glass and other ceramic materials together for use in glazes, stains and on-glaze enamels. Substances which are soluble or toxic can be rendered safe for use by incorporating into frits.

Fused: A glaze which has melted to form a smooth, glassy surface.

Fusibility: The ability of a ceramic material to melt.

Greenware: Unfired pottery that is air dry.

Grog: Clay that has been fired and ground to varying granule sizes. Grog is added to clay bodies to provide texture, and strength when throwing or handbuilding, to assist drying, reduce shrinkage and increase firing strength.

Hue: A hue is a pure colour, without additions of black, white or grey.

Kiln wash: Also known as batwash, this consists of a refractory mixture of calcinated alumina and kaolin which is painted onto kiln shelves to protect them from glaze spills.

Leatherhard: A stage of drying at which clay is stiff but still contains moisture. At this stage, additions may be joined with slip, ware may be trimmed or carved, and decorated with slips or underglazes.

Majolica: A style of decorated pottery with metal oxides or stains painted on top of an unfired, white tin-opacified glaze which fires to earthenware temperatures.

Refractory: The ability of a ceramic material to resist high temperatures (heat) without melting.

Resist: An area on the clay surface masked with wax or a paper cutout, over which colouring is added to achieve a stencil effect.

Scoring: Roughening the surface of clay with a pin tool or a toothbrush. With slip added, this enables other pieces of clay to be joined to the surface, or two surfaces to be joined together.

Set up: When a pot is allowed to 'set up' it means the pot is left to stand until clay, slip or glaze slightly stiffens or dries out.

Sgraffito: A decorating technique involving scratching through a layer of slip to expose the clay body or a different colour of slip underneath. A variety of tools may be employed, from fingers on very wet slip to bamboo skewers, a ballpoint pen or a pin tool on slip that has set up, or dental tools on slip that is dry (wear a mask!).

Slake: To make clay wet by immersing it in water.

Slip: Liquid clay applied to the surface of a clay body. Slip can be coloured for varying decorative effects. Light slip may be painted or poured onto a dark clay body then scratched or combed through. Slip may be trailed onto the surface of a pot with a device called a slip trailer.

Slip-casting: Forms may be repeated by pouring into a plaster mould, which absorbs the moisture in the slip, allowing the clay to form a 'skin' or thin wall of clay. Surplus slip is poured away and the form is left to dry before removing from the mould. Casting slip differs from the normal slip in that a deflocculant must be added to the slip. This means less water content is required in the slip, therefore there is less shrinkage and greater flexibility to the slip.

Slurry: A thicker mixture of clay and water (slip) which is used when joining clay together.

Underglaze: Coloured pigments mixed with ceramic materials which are painted or sprayed onto raw or bisque ware before a clear glaze is put on top. Used for colourful decoration of clay.

Vitrification: Firing clay to the point at which it reaches a glassy state.

Wadding: Bits of soft clay, usually made of fireclay, used to level kiln shelves, or stack pots for glaze firing in the kiln.

Warping: Deforming of a pot which is caused by uneven shrinkage. Warping can occur if work is dried or fired unevenly or too quickly. Many factors exacerbate warping—insufficient wedging of clay, uneven clay walls, high shrinkage, thin rims, etc.

Further Reading

Berensohn, P., *Finding One's Way with Clay—Pinched Pottery and the Colour of Clay*, Simon and Schuster, New York, 1972.

Casson, M., *The Craft of the Potter—A Practical Guide to Making Pottery*, British Broadcasting Corporation, London, 1977.

Cowley, D., *Molded and Slip Cast Pottery and Ceramics*, Batsford, London 1978.

Daly, G., *Glazes and Glazing Techniques*, Kangaroo Press, Kenthurst, Australia, 1995.

Fournier, R., *Illustrated Dictionary of Practical Pottery*, Van Nostrand–Reinhold, New York, 1973.

Fraser, H., *Electric Kilns and Firing*, Pitman Publishing Ltd, London, 1979.

McMeekin, I., *Notes for Potters in Australia—Raw Materials and Clay Bodies*, NSW University Press, Kensington, Australia, 1985.

Rogers, M., *Mary Rogers on Pottery and Porcelain—A Handbuilder's Approach*, Alphabooks, England, 1984.

Index